NOT
So Dumb

Famed director Alfred Hitchcock fearlessly takes a little tea with the King of Beasts. (Photo by Clarence Sinclair Bull)

NOT
So Dumb

THE LIFE AND TIMES
OF THE ANIMAL ACTORS

Raymond Lee

CASTLE BOOKS ★ **NEW YORK**

© 1970 by A. S. Barnes and Co., Inc.

Library of Congress Catalogue Card Number: 69-15770

This Edition Published by Arrangement with A. S. Barnes & Co., Inc.

SBN: 498 07525 7

Printed in the United States of America

For Bill,
my favorite parrot and,
his mistress, Stella Rae,
my favorite voice coach
who talked me into writing this book
about the film animals . . .

ACKNOWLEDGMENTS

ACADEMY OF MOTION PICTURE ARTS AND SCIENCES
AMERICAN HUMANE ASSOCIATION—JOHN ECCLESTON, HAROLD MELNIKER
WALT DISNEY PRODUCTIONS—DICK MCKAY
IVAN TORS FILMS, INC.—IVAN TORS
COUNTY OF LOS ANGELES—DEPARTMENT OF PARKS & RECREATION
MACFADDEN-BARTELL CORPORATION—MARK J. GREENBERG
LETTERS TO STRONGHEART—J. ALLEN BOONE
TWO REELS AND A CRANK—ALBERT E. SMITH WITH PHIL A. KOURY
CHARLIE CHAPLIN—THEODORE HUFF
WILD ANIMAL ACTORS—H. M. & F. M. CHRISTESON
THE WEST OF YESTERDAY—TOM MIX
ART RUSH, INC.—W. ARTHUR RUSH, PRESIDENT
MOSAIC MAGAZINE—GUS SPATHIAS
LOS ANGELES TIMES—DICK MAIN
LOS ANGELES EXAMINER
THE TRIANGLE WEEKLY
SATURDAY EVENING POST
CINEMA AMERICA—DIRECTOR B. C. VAN HECKE
LOWELL E. REDELINGS
JOEL SAYRE
JOHN REESE
WILLIAM CAMPBELL
VERNON DENT
LOUISE FAZENDA
MINTA DURFEE ARBUCKLE
GUNNARD NELSON
RICHARD HUDSON
VIVIEN BURGOON—FOR MRS. ARBUCKLE PORTRAIT
DIANE GOODRICH—SPECIAL PHOTOGRAPHIC REPRODUCTION

"Canine Movie Fans—1915 Vintage" reprinted by permission of *Photoplay* Magazine, July 1915. Published by MacFadden-Bartell Corporation.

"A Thousand Pounds of Dynamite," from *My Life East and West,* by William S. Hart, published by Houghton Mifflin Co., Riverside Press, Cambridge. Reprinted by permission.

"Strongheart" reprinted by permission of J. Allen Boone.

"Miracle of the Dolphins" by Ivan Tors, reprinted by permission of Mr. Tors.

Chapter 35 reprinted by permission of the *Los Angeles Examiner.*

CONTENTS

1 FADE-IN

On the whim of Lillian Gish, the silent screen's first lady, I began acting before Hollywood's cameras in 1915. My mother's baby-sitter had gone off for the day with the boy next door so I tagged along to the Fine Arts Studio where she worked in the wardrobe department while David Wark Griffith was making cinema history with *Birth of a Nation*.

My love of human actors walked hand in hand with my love of their animal counterparts as I played with them or became an ardent fan. In the years that followed sometimes I didn't know which was the bigger object of my affections.

For the past fifty years the roster of animal stars has sparkled on the theatre marquees around the globs in lights as bright as those used for two-legged luminaries.

Mack Sennett's Menagerie, Teddy the Great Dane, Pepper the alley-cat, Anna May the elephant, and the lions Numa and Duke, Strongheart and Rin Tin Tin the fabled German Police canines, Tom Mix's wonder horse Tony, Lassie, Francis the mule, Rhubarb, the Disney Dogs, to name a few.

Who built the movie ark?

In 1889 Tom Edison's first successful flicker showed Will Dickson with his hand resting on a horse being fitted for a shoe.

Horse Eating Hay in 1897 launched the Sigmund Lubin Company.

Shoulder to shoulder with Pickford, Fairbanks and Chaplin the animals helped to turn the "jumping shadows" into the world's top entertainment medium.

Some gave their lives.

In the Twenties, Rin Tin Tin ran to the rescue not only on the screen but as a box-office bonanza that saved the struggling Warner Brothers from bankruptcy.

So if the not so dumb animals sometimes have acted like humans, don't blame them too much. Remember what poet Sir Thomas Browne sung:

"Man is a noble animal . . ."

Why shouldn't he be imitated by other animals?

Now, who was the film Noah who pinned the first star on the second ark?

2 NOAH'S SECOND ARK

How to foil the villain was the theme of all early flickers, and how to do it each time with a different climax was the problem.

When a young writer brought a script to Albert E. Smith, titular head of New York Vitagraph, in which a dog bested the villain and saved the hero from death, Smith paid him the unheard price of—$10.00. But 1912 was the time for daring deeds.

Smith began testing canine actors to play the difficult part. He found no four-legged thespians. But Smith's career had been ground out the hard way—behind a newsreel camera. He had photographed transport wagons crossing a ford over the Tulgela River in South Africa during the Boer war of 1899. Before President McKinley was shot on September 6, 1901, he had captured him on film. And when Teddy Roosevelt charged up San Juan Hill Smith's camera was on his heels. The tests went on.

One of Smith's greatest discoveries was Vitagraph's leading star, beautiful Florence Turner, and it was only fitting that she should be the one to discover a dog for him.

One morning, as Florence alighted from her car in front of the Brooklyn Studios to perform in Charles Dickens's classic, *A Tale of Two Cities,* she paused to watch a young man playing with a beautiful collie.

She seemed almost human: He'd throw a stick and she'd bring it back; she would play dead on command; she would sit up and throw her legs around his neck.

"I'm Florence Turner, young man."

"Yes, I know," he said shyly. "My name is Larry Trimble."

"Do you also know Mr. Smith is looking for a dog to star in a series?"

As the young man nodded, Miss Turner ran her hand through the collie's thick ruff.

"What do you call her?"

"Jean."

"Well, Jeannie-girl, how would you like to be in pictures?"

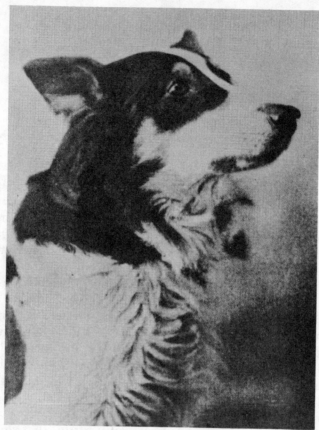

Jean, the first dog star.

Later, inside the studio:

"Well, Mr. Trimble, if your dog can untie knots and free the hero's hands and feet, he's got the part."

"He's a she, Albert," Miss Turner whispered.

"We can fake the other business he—I mean, she—can't do."

"Mr. Smith," Larry Trimble said firmly, "you won't have to fake anything; Jean will do anything I ask her."

One of the prop hands quickly tied Larry up and as all watched, Jean almost instantly freed her master and won a round of applause.

Shaking Larry's hand, Smith said:

"I have no written contracts with my players. Just a handshake. We are a family. If we haven't that kind of trust we haven't anything. I'll start you and Jean at $25.00 a week. If the series catches on we'll soon raise that."

It caught on and the first dog star rose in the celluloid sky.

Flushed with the tremendous success Smith plunged into the growing animal craze with the gusto of a big game hunter.

But he had another big gamer on his tail, Colonel William Selig of Selig Polyscope Company. A race was on between Brooklyn and Chicago and a few long shots were not far behind the favorites.

Smith hired two traveling menageries, more than one hundred animals ranging from the king of beasts to the rarest monkey. They were housed in tents, garages, shacks and the basement of the Flatbush Studio.

As with all pioneers, the Vitagraph Noah's venture into an African jungle transplant had many startling results.

One movie plot involved a gentleman returning from India with a tiger as a pet. The tiger was allowed to roam the house like a domestic pet. The gentleman's fiancee didn't relish this and complications naturally followed. The lady or the tiger?

The climax of a party celebrating the announcement of the wedding had the tiger nonchalantly sashaying among the guests. It ended quite differently from the high-priced script ($25.00).

As the big scene was lined up, the tiger suddenly turned on his trainer, sinking his teeth in his neck. While actors screamed, fainted and scattered, Smith's brother, Victor, who as a precaution had stationed himself behind the camera, killed the enraged beast with a blast from his .30–.30.

But the trainer, whose life had been saved, sued Vitagraph for killing his tiger. As the movie Noah signed a $500.00 check he pondered the future of wild animals in his productions.

Colonel Selig just smiled as he heard of the lawsuit and filmed the first serial, *The Adventures of Kathlyn*. The film featured lovely Kathlyn Williams, being chased each week by lions, leopards and rhinos through episode after episode. And the lines at the box office grew longer and longer.

Would Albert E. Smith surrender the lead now?

The soft-spoken man of action opened his Bible, and after reading the chapter on Daniel and the Lions' Den, he decided to film it.

Fred ("Bing") Thompson was the director; and being a man of caution, he decided to shoot the famous scene in the lions' den at the end of the picture. As he said to his boss, "just in case one of the cats might take a bite out of our Daniel."

On the last day of shooting Albert Smith received a rush call to the den set. He hurried on stage expecting the worst. Thompson quickly guided him to one side, explaining that Daniel was refusing to work with the lions. He was scared stiff.

Smith motioned for the animal trainer to join them.

"Joe, any of your cats ever chew up anybody?"

"Mr. Smith, them cats is o.k. Anybody can work with 'em long

Albert E. Smith and Daniel's lions.

as they don't make a fast move. Let the lions move first."

"Do you feed them before they perform?"

"Feed 'em? They get better than you'd get at the Waldorf Astoria!"

Smith turned and walked briskly into the den. Surrounded by a high wire enclosure it protected outsiders; but the insider was trapped. The company watched in disbelief.

As Noah might have, Smith looked at the lions. The lions looked back. Slowly one of the great males ambled over to him. The lion stared up. Smith stared down. The king of beasts sniffed his shoe-tops, slowly raising his massive head to the man's belt line. Smith could never recall why he did it, but he put his hand on the lion's head. The lion blinked and then rubbed his head against Smith's leg. Slowly again the great cat turned around and sauntered back to the other six and slumped down with a sigh heard all over the stage. The head of Vitagraph, head high and looking like a king of men, stalked off the electrified set.

Ten tense minutes passed in his office as Smith waited for word from the set. Had he gone too far? What if the lion didn't like the Daniel-actor's smell? He was about to send someone over when a prop boy entered and handed his boss the following note:

"Daniel is emoting all over the den and I think the lions are loving it. What an inspiration you were! Bing . . ."

The picture was a smashing hit. No holding Noah Smith now.

In *Wild Animals At Large,* a rather dubious title following the off-camera hijinks; a traveling menagerie was featured. On a ten-acre field in New Jersey the drama reached a shock peak in a spectacular wreck; shattered cages and screaming animals spilled all over the countryside.

A fence of heavy planking encircled the area. But again the unexpected crossed the Vitagrapher's path and almost set back the animal actors to the mild days of Jean the collie.

Setting up for the big scene a young leopard leaped over the enclosure and bounded off to a nearby village.

In the town barbershop a customer was being shaved. Suddenly the shaver looked up and couldn't believe what he saw—a leopard loping into his parlor. He dashed out the back door. As the shavee looked up to see what had happened to the shaver and saw the leopard leaping at him, he fainted. But as the snarling cat dug his claws into his leg he woke up pronto and his wild screams brought the keepers to the rescue with ropes and nets.

When all things were restored to order, Smith debated calling off the whole thing. How could he keep these wild animals in tow? What if somebody got killed?

Suddenly Vitagraph's adjuster stepped into the tent where Smith had quartered himself.

"Don't tell me," he almost moaned.

"Mr. Smith I settled all damages for the sum of fifty dollars, believe it or not."

Albert E. Smith wanted to believe it. As he looked over the release from the barber he called in his assistants directing them to proceed with operation: wild animals.

While the picture was in the cutting stage Albert E. Smith was served with a paper that stated the barbershop customer was suing Vitagraph for the leopard attack on him. As Smith read further he was puzzled: The litigation was not for injury to his leg.

Some time after the horrifying episode the man's thick black head of curly hair had turned white and a few days later fell out—all of it. He was now completely bald!

The settlement was for $3,000; the *largest claim* ever against Vitagraph and its animal actors. Albert E. Smith again pondered shutting the cage on his wild ones while hearing rumors that Colonel Selig was going strong with animal antics that defied imagination.

The newspapers headlined the lawsuit and every place he went he heard people talking about the bald incident. It was the laugh of the times.

Smith called a conference.

With $3,000 involved, everybody was laughing but Vitagraph.

There must be some way to turn this card in their favor: Why not put the incident in the film as comedy relief to the wreck? Why not? So the scene was faked and put in *Wild Animals At Large*. Audiences roared at the barbershop sequence. The only complaints came from the few people who had leopards as pets and denied that the leg-chewing scene could have taken place.

Although the story has no basis in fact, some people say that Albert E. Smith sent a package to Colonel Selig. When the esteemed Colonel opened it, he found a leopard's skin. There are those who claim that the skin hung on the wall of the Colonel's office for many years.

Naturally, Mr. Noah doubled production on his animal adventures.

The courageous pioneer has written and told many fascinating tales about his animal stars and of course he had one favorite which is best described in his own words:

"We planned a movie called, *A Horse of a Different Color*, a simple tale of a horse dealer who owns a dirty white horse whom no one would buy. He paints her brown but makes the mistake of using cold-water paint. The purchaser, giving his new animal a bath, is shocked to observe freshets of brown paint streaming off the horse on to the ground.

"Even though it was an era when horses were plentiful, we had difficulty finding a white horse that fit both our budget and script specifications.

"Finally, near Coney Island, our prop boy, Walter Ackerman, found an undertaker with a horse he said he'd lend us for a few dollars. He told the prop boy the horse was worth $25.00. We sent back word that we would pay that amount if anything serious happened to the animal plus his fee.

"As per script, the horse was white through the first part of the story, and when it came time for her to change color our property department diligently provided the horse dealer with brown paint. Brown *oil* paint! Naturally the paint wouldn't wash off and the climax was ruined.

"We quickly sent out a search party for another white horse and the prop boy trudged disconsolately back to the undertaker, leading the horse with the *permanent* paint job.

"The undertaker was furious when the prop boy said, 'We haven't hurt her, sir. I think she looks better than when she was white.'

"The undertaker shouted back, 'I can't use a brown horse in my funeral services. White or black, yes, but never brown!'

"When the boy returned and told the story we instructed him

to try and settle for ten dollars but if the undertaker threatened a lawsuit to give him the twenty-five.

"To the boy's surprise the undertaker was all smiles when he returned and patted the lad on the shoulder and pointed down the street where a man was leading the brown mare.

" 'I tried to sell that old horse for $25.00 when she was white and now that she's brown I got a whopping fifty. Tell your Mr. Vitagraph, he owes me nothing and I am most grateful . . .' "

In March, 1948, at the Twentieth Annual Academy Awards Ceremonies, the Motion Picture Academy of Arts and Sciences honored several pioneers, and Albert E. Smith was among those. The inscription on the base of his Oscar read:

"One of the small group of pioneers whose belief in a new medium, and whose contributions to its development, blazed the trail along which the motion picture has progressed, in their life-time, from obscurity to world-wide acclaim."

At the Carthay Circle Theatre in Los Angeles, 1951, the first PATSY awards, PATSY meaning, Picture Animal Top Star of the Year, was held, and Francis the talking mule received the initial award.

"Man is a noble animal . . ."

Why shouldn't he be imitated by other animals?

3 A TWENTY-FOOT FIDO

In 1914 the Lubin Company was shooting, on the outskirts of New York City, *The Eternal Sacrifice,* a story of mother-love throughout the ages; it starred Ormi Hawley.

Ormi's career was hanging in the balance. Her last film, *The Splendid Romance,* in which she had played opposite the world's greatest tenor, had been a shelved flop because the magnificent voice of Enrico Caruso could not be heard.

As director James Terwillinger called for a new scene Ormi, who had always admitted to being a nature girl, strolled off into the surrounding woods. Stumbling onto a small traveling circus, she wandered up to a cage where a massive python lay coiled up like a pile of hoops—snoring hoops.

Slowly she unlatched the cage and gently stroked the sleeper. Suddenly out of the mass of fireman's hose a head rose, the coils flowing around it like green waves. Ormi's hand resembled a live pigeon in the filtered light.

But as the lovely Ormi-vision floated out of the afternoon haze the monstrous snake turned goggle-eyed, and with the enthusiasm of a Christmas package-wrapper, began tieing up her loveliness.

At this embracing moment one of Terwillinger's assistants, looking for the star, came upon the pair. He fainted dead away.

As Ormi staggered back on the set, weighed down to her ankles in python, everyone but the director took off.

Terwillinger, stroking the snake's head, said prophetically:

"We must have him in the picture. He will be a sensation. He'll make the public forget Caruso, believe me, Ormi."

The circus owner arrived at this momentous juncture and was asked the king size convoluter's name.

"When I bought him they said they called him Fido."

Director and star exchanged looks as he said this.

"Don't ask me why. I tried changing his name but he never answered to anything but Fido—even when I called him for dinner."

One of the returning crew quipped, "Fido? Is that because he likes Fidoes instead of chicken for his main course?"

The 20-foot Fido.

Fido fell in love with the clicking camera as much as with Ormi. Everytime Terwillinger said "Camera! Action!" the snake glowed and seemed almost human as he followed directions.

The day Ormi and Fido parted company even Fido had tears in his eyes.

Terwillinger begged the owner to wait until the film was shown. He was sure Fido would be a star. He had several plots in mind. The little big-topper shook his head and said he didn't live on promises. So the wagons rolled over the horizon.

When *The Eternal Sacrifice* was released the sight of the beautiful girl in the coils of the undulating python caused near riots. As fast as fans ran out, others ran in. The country-wide distribution proved that the public loved the amazing duo.

A hurry up call by Sigmund Lubin sent talent scouts scurrying to the four corners of the U.S. in search of Fido. After months of fruitless hunting Lubin called in his human hounds.

Many stories were written about Fido and his disappearance. To this day he remains one of the early flickers' most intriguing mysteries.

What a performance he would have given as the Serpent in the Garden of Eden! With Ormi as Eve, of course.

4 PROPS

He was found whimpering one rainy morning in a clothes basket by Bill Buskirk, head of the Property Department, the genial stage boss of the Fine Arts Studio in Hollywood. Bill called his find Props, and all hands promptly adopted the puppy as their mascot. But not for long. Soon everyone from D. W. Griffith on down was seeking the favor of the brown-eyed foundling and he was given the run of the lot.

As the 1915 epics unreeled Props displayed a quite remarkable intelligence and understanding. Some other dog might have just nosed around the film factory. Not Props. He must have realized how much he was needed. Mapping out a schedule like all other movie people working under the Fine Arts banner, he never was off an hour in his routine, except when acting before the cameras himself.

Every morning the little dog met Dad Thoren, the gateman, as he opened the studio to traffic. He gave a wagging, individual greeting to both the walking and riding personnel. Dad swore he could tell time because at nine o'clock sharp Props would always tail off for his morning tour of the companies in production.

He would watch a scene or two being shot, receive a pat on the head or a mouth-watering sweet, and then he'd go on to the next stage. As the companies broke for lunch he'd sit outside the little bungalow-cafe where the actors and crew ate. No dog had ever eaten so well no matter how big his salary.

His after-lunch siesta always took place in the confines of the Property Department. He paid special tribute to Bill Buskirk by snoozing under his desk.

Oftentimes the prop hands would play a quick game of poker or roll the dice following their lunch. And on occasion, a snooping "efficiency expert," an unexplained agent who tried to save money for the studio, while making an inspection tour would catch and reprimand them. Second offenders were sometimes fired.

But this was B.P.—Before Props. When a game started, Props

would suddenly unwind himself from his siesta and park outside the building, seeming to resume his snooze. After a while the boys heard a growl; then a bark; then a series of barks. Curious, a player would sneak a look out front. Ducking back inside, his whispered warning would break up the game. Props was giving the old heave-ho to an efficiency expert.

How the little spotter ever took up this guard duty nobody could ever imagine, but Props never failed his post and not a hand ever got the axe for flirting with Lady Luck on studio time.

I always remember a big moment at Miss Sarah P. McClung's school for us Triangle Kiddies. As school let out Props would always be there with a jumping, kissing greeting and a begging for some playtime. This lasted about ten minutes, after which he would hightail it for the stages again. No matter how we coaxed he never would play more than ten minutes.

At the end of the day he waited outside the projection room where the rushes, the day's shooting, were run off. Sometimes a director who favored him, like Paul Powell, would take him in and he'd watch the screen as attentive as any human.

No one knew where Props slept. He could be discovered in a variety of spots: One time he'd be in a luxurious bed used in a Bessie Barriscale society drama, another time in the dressing room of Dorothy Gish, who taught him many of his amazing tricks. Once Griffith found him curled up in his favorite office chair. As a bevy of assistants waited for an explosion, D. W., father of films, just smiled and patted Props's head and sat in another chair.

How Props entered pictures was almost as story-book as his appearance in the clothes basket.

The Triangle Kiddies, of which I was now a Junior member, were working with beautiful Norma Talmadge in *Children in the House*. Props, paying his daily visit, just sat watching. Baby Charles Spofford had a big scene coming up. At two years Baby Charles could act the pants off of any of us.

In the scene with Baby Charles we plop him into a wagon to get rid of him. As we wander off he falls asleep. Suddenly as he shifts the wagon starts rolling toward a nearby gully. Norma Talmadge enters just in time to rescue him.

On direction from Christy Cabanne, the scene progressed. We put Baby Charles in the wagon, he closed his eyes, the prop men started pulling the wires attached to the wagon. The wagon moved slowly downhill. But just as Miss Talmadge entered she tripped and fell over a tree branch. Everyone froze. The wagon hit a rock, broke loose from the wires, headed for the gully. Props suddenly dashed from behind the camera and flung himself in front of the wagon. It stopped inches short of the gully.

Charles Spofford with Props.

As Mrs. Grover held her priceless Baby Charles in her arms, hero Props licked away his tears and won himself a career. Fortunately, cameraman Frank Good had kept grinding and the exciting action was on film.

Props, while viewing the rushes, was jumping up and down barking like he didn't recognize himself but later, when Christy Cabanne explained it was himself, the little dog sat quiet and watched a rerun.

There was no stopping Props now. Everyone wanted him for a picture. And no one had to pay a dime for his services! A truly unique setup in high-salaried Hollywood.

He ran the gamut of emotions from comedy to tragedy with such top box-office winners as DeWolfe Hopper, of stage fame, in his first film, *Casey At the Bat*; the Gish sisters; H. B. Warner in some cloak and dagger thrillers; and he was once loaned to William S. Hart for a shoot-em-upper.

But his greatest role everyone agreed was in a Dorothy Gish classic called, *The Little Yank*. George Siegmann, remembered for his villainy in Griffith's *Birth of a Nation*, directed. It was quite common in the early days for actors to do several chores, thus revealing their multiple talents.

The story had a Civil War background. Siegmann wanted to show some of the pathos Griffith always incorporated in his films. He tried several ideas and then sat down for a conference.

Props was sitting on Dorothy Gish's lap eating peanuts. Suddenly she jumped up and peanuts and Props fell every which way. She rushed over to her director and explained her inspiration. Siegmann shrugged his shoulders. At this point he'd try anything. Anything was to be Props.

The scene took place on a Southern battlefield. The hero, Elmer Clifton, later the director who discovered Clara Bow, shoots at what he thinks is another soldier hiding behind a bush. It turns out to be a dog—Props. He is so overcome with humiliation and pity he makes a splint for the dog's leg and hides him from further harm on the explosive countryside.

Impressed with the canine's natural talent, Siegmann called for a close-up as Props first tried to walk on his splint. Sniffles, tears and applause, plus kisses showered by Dorothy, crowned the foundling's acting. Following this performance Siegmann naturally built up Props's part.

Sometime later, while a few of us kids were looking for fun between lulls in shooting on a Wallace Reid film, we found Props curled up in a wheelbarrow. We tried to get his attention with a game of catch. He just lay curled up. Nothing we did roused him. Finally we cradled him out of the wheelbarrow and set him on the ground and rolled the ball a few feet away. Slowly he went for the ball, his right leg held up like it was broken. One of the girls started bawling that Props was going to die.

Madame Sul-te-Wan, the first Negro actress to make a name in flickers with the help of D. W. Griffith, happened on the scene and after soothing the little girl's tears quickly gave Props the once-over. Her huge brown eyes narrowed to slits and her usually jovial face wore a mask of gloom. She said something in an African tongue that always mystified everyone and then in English.

"Children, something funny got hold of this hound-dog. Ain't got a broken bone or twisted hair in his leg or any part of him. Still he keeps holding his leg up like it's in a splint. Looks like our Props has been hexed."

We all stared low-lipped as Madame's deep voice sounded what sounded like doom. Even the morning sun had a cloud over it though there wasn't a cloud in the sky.

George Siegmann emerged from the stage into this bewilderment. He stopped, stared, and began guffawing like he was watching the Keystone Kops.

Madame barged up, feathers flying.

"What's so funny, Mr. George Siegmann? Our dog Props is hexed and he needs help and you belly-laugh."

Siegmann's laugh hid a lump in his throat.

"Madame, don't you know what's wrong with that ham? Remember his performance in my last picture? You know he stole it blind—even from Dorothy Gish. Well, guess he thinks it's his best bet from now on. Look at him holding up his leg like he's still on the battle-field!"

As he backed away, stifling another laugh, we all stared at Props holding his leg up. Millard Webb, the assistant director on our picture, called us back for a scene. As we filed onto the stage there was Props holding up his leg with Madame looking on like *she* was hexed.

Everybody on the lot tried to cure Props of his "hex." He was given the choicest meats and bones, a brand new pipe for him to do his "Sherlock Holmes" routine with, even a collar with jewels in it from the Gish girls. He still hobbled around.

As Madame walked through the gates one morning and saw Props there with one leg "splinted," she grabbed him up in her arms and headed for David Wark Griffith's office.

Explaining the "hex," Griffith interrupted:

"Put him on my desk, Madame."

Griffith stared down at Props. Props stared up. The little dog began quivering all over, even his tail. Griffith's voice, which could rumble five thousand extras into a surging mob scene, thundered the walls of his office.

"Props, you must stop this farce!"

The little dog was now quivering even down to his toes. Madame reached to pick him up, Griffith frowned, Madame retreated.

"Props, I enjoyed your performance in *The Little Yank* very much. But that's all over. It may be your best to date. But we are all sure you have more, maybe better."

The great director and the little dog looked as only man and animal can look at each other.

"Props, as the head of the Fine Arts Studio and your employer, I ask you to please put your foot down and be our dog again."

Again that look between man and dog. Slowly the paw lowered and the tail wagged. Mr. Griffith put his hand on the animal's head as Madame mumbled something in Swahili.

5 LEO AND THE GOVERNOR

During the filming of Griffith's million dollar 1916 colossus, *Intolerance*, which depicted man's inhumanity to man through the ages, Hiram T. Johnson, Governor of California, was a luncheon guest.

Afterward Griffith showed him the monstrous Babylonian sets he had built in which Belshazzar's Victory Feast over his defeat of the invader Cyrus would be celebrated with a cast of 10,000.

Griffith escorted the Governor to a chair near the camera and proceeded to direct a scene in the slave market where beautiful girls were sold to the highest bidder.

Governor Johnson, who had broken the railroad stranglehold on the Golden State, proved his courage wasn't confined only to politics.

Leo, a nine-year-old veteran of pioneer films and a pet of D. W.'s, paced back and forth in his cage waiting to emote. Somehow he loosened the side of his enclosure and shoved his way between the bars and meandered up to the Governor, who was enthralled with the scene. While hundreds of actors and assistants stared horrified, Leo dropped his head in Johnson's lap.

Griffith held up his hands for quiet and motioned that no one should make a move. As he turned to tip-toe behind the massive cat, he went wide-eyed as he heard the Governor's voice break the stifling tension.

"Nice old fellow, nice old Leo." Lifting the lion's head, he patted it and as the big cat let out a soft growl that ended in an engulfing yawn, the Governor continued, "Lose another tooth, old boy?"

Griffith's hand was on Leo's collar and a quick apology was on his lips. The Governor smiled broadly, and pulling off a few lion hairs from his sleeve, replied, "Sir, I've petted babies and dogs and anything that walked in my campaign to Sacramento. What's a lion but in line of duty?"

A bevy of publicity men hovered around the Governor's car as he drove off the huge set.

"Afraid of Leo? Gentlemen, you can see for yourselves he's just an overgrown pussycat. What really scared me was watching Mr. Griffith direct those mob scenes. You know, folks can get out of temper or step and then anything can happen. But that Griffith voice would stop a tidal wave." As his car pulled away slowly, "I'll take governing a state any day to directing a spectacle like this *Intolerance*."

Of course not many outside of the Griffith inner circle knew that Leo was almost toothless and clawless and too old to harm anyone unless he slipped and fell on them. He was really just another gag Griffith loved to pull on notable visitors and friends. But what about the Governor? Was he so brave or did he suspect the gag and just go along with it?

6 SUSIE

D. W. Griffith championed the lost cause in most of his masterful films. In 1924 he produced a picture partially shot in Germany, *Isn't Life Wonderful?*. It starred Neil Hamilton and Carol Dempster, supported by native actors, etching a beautiful and bitter drama of Germany's struggle for food following World War I.

When Griffith returned from Europe to finish the film at his Mamaroneck Studios in New York, newsmen quickly gathered to question him about whether he had brought back any foreign discoveries. As the father of discoveries he smiled and replied: "Yes, a German actress of extraordinary talent. Would you like to meet her?"

The reporters pressed forward.

Draping a plaid overcoat over his shoulders, tapping his hat as if it were a cane, he warned the lady didn't speak a word of English and let them out of his office into a backyard where trees and bushes framed a sylvan scene.

One of the reporters caught a flying sleeve of D. W.'s coat.

"What's the young lady's name, Mr. Griffith?"

Griffith stopped with exaggerated attention trying to pull his overcoat into the shape of a cape, never having quite forgotten his first ventures in flickers had been as an actor.

"I'm trying something different with my new discovery. Something simple. You know, how confusing some foreign names can be. I'm calling her—Susie!"

The yard broadened. They passed a truck loaded with hay. More lawn and suddenly a crate emblazoned by the morning sunlight before which the noted director-producer ceremoniously halted.

Down on one knee, he lifted a shutter in the box. He whispered something in German. The newsmen pressed forward. Shyly a Plymouth Rock hen poked her head into the light and then, as Griffith coaxed, strutted front and center.

The newsmen blinked and pencils scratched on pads.

"Susie is a Plymouth Rock from a village near Berlin. Fate let her wander into a scene I was shooting near a humble homestead. From the minute I saw her I knew she wasn't an ordinary hen.

Susie and D. W. Griffith.

Friendly and intelligent, she recognized me as a man of authority. At the slightest encouragement she would throw back her head and sing lustily. It wasn't just cackling, it was a merry tune worthy of Humperdinck. You see, gentlemen, Susie is a rare bird, a 'crowing hen' as the British and New Englander country folk call them. To me she's a singer, not a crower."

The big news was filling the pads.

"One day Susie's owner showed up. By that time I had used her in so many sequences I had to have her for other shots to be made in America. I offered to buy Susie. The sum was large in German marks. Her owner wept. But despite the poverty of the man and his family of three, he couldn't part with her.

"I compromised by agreeing to hire Susie at a monthly salary and promised when the picture was finished to ship her back to Germany."

Susie was nibbling corn Griffith had taken from a pocket.

"Would you like to hear her sing?"

The newsmen nodded.

As she nuzzled his palm, Griffith again whispered in German, stroking her neck several times. Suddenly Susie sensed the moment, threw back her head and belted out a high C any Prima Donna would have been proud of.

7

A "LUCKY DOG" WHO WAS A BEAR

Director James Young, to produce the 1916 *Heart of the Blue Ridge*, starring his beautiful wife, Clara Kimball Young, hiked his company into the North Carolina mountains, in the region of Bat Cove, the feud center, to insure authentic background.

Clara loved the people and the mountains. And they loved her. How she had them gasping at her amazing marksmanship!

At the end of the first day's shooting, James informed his wife that the property department had forgotten to bring along a trained bear for the humor episodes. It was too late to have one brought out from Hollywood. He guessed they'd have to cut the sequence.

Clara said, "Since you're not using me tomorrow, I'll go hunting for your bear."

Young didn't answer knowing full well his wife's ability to do almost anything.

The Chimney Rock Falls had a drop of one thousand feet. Like the flowing tresses of a beautiful woman they tumbled down the mountainside. After watching this awe-inspiring sight Clara decided to go wading in one of the many pools formed below the falls.

Knee-deep in chilling water Clara looked up as a young brown bear lumbered out of the brush and stood staring at her. They faced each other for a long moment and then Clara motioned him toward her. As though he'd known her all of his life he plunged into the pool.

For almost ten minutes the lady and the bear frolicked. When the lady had enough she waded ashore. The bear followed. After drying herself she headed for camp. The bear followed.

The mountaineers were open-mouthed as they watched Clara feed her newly found companion. They dubbed him—"Lucky Dog," which he became, as Clara showed her find to her husband.

"Didn't I tell you I'd find a bear. He'll do anything I ask him. He's adorable."

Lucky Dog acted like a seasoned ham. The bear stole every scene from his human players. He was a natural. Director Young became

"Lucky Dog" and Clara Kimball Young.

so enthusiastic about the backwoods discovery he thought of doing a series in Hollywood about what happens to a bear who is taken to the glamor city. Clara just smiled as James raved on and on.

The last morning of production, sipping coffee before the trek back out of the mountains to cinemaland, Clara said gently as she filled her husband's cup, "Jimmy, we really can't take 'Lucky' back with us."

"But, honey, I've written the studio about him. Practically everything's settled."

"I know. But he belongs here. He might even sicken and die in our uncertain California climate. How would you feel then?"

Young frowned.

Clara's lovely eyes misted as if they had looked too long at the Chimney Rock Falls.

"I love him as much as you do. And I am sure he would become quite an animal star. But because we love him we should give him up. Here he has all of nature to live and love for. What could we give him but a career—and a cage?"

James Young smiled away his disappointment. Clara reached for his hand saying, "Come, let's say goodbye to him." The dynamic director who never shirked anything shook his head and mumbled something about getting the company on the trail.

But a few moments later he watched his wife lead the brown fellow into a thicket and say goodbye to him as if it were the most natural thing for a lady and a bear to do.

He whispered into a crisp breeze,

"Happy hibernation, 'Lucky Dog.' "

8 $5,000 WORTH OF PEPPER

Mack Sennett was the undisputed King of Comedy. No monarch ever ruled a zanier domain in which Charlie Chaplin, Mabel Normand, Fatty Arbuckle, Louise Fazenda and many others, with honor guard from the Keystone Kops, tickled the funnybone of the world.

But these peerless laugh-makers had to share the custard pie roster with King Mack's reliables—his beloved animal actors.

When a comedy lagged or the gags didn't come off, Mack shouted for his sure-fire brigade—Pepper the alley-cat, Teddy the Great Dane, Anna May the elephant or his team of lions, Numa and Duke. His second line of gloom-busters ranged from John Brown, a teddy bear grizzly to rattlesnakes and a white mouse named Frederich Wilhelm; for a novelty there was Carrie Nation, a chicken of dubious origin.

The keystone zoo boasted its Bernhardts and Barrymores but none outshined Pepper, whose career was a Cinderella story all her own—from alley to film throne. Sennett once refused $5,000 for her, backing the buyer out of his office, protesting that it wasn't even a down payment on his star attraction.

Eddie Cline, directing a slapstick caper with Ford Sterling and Louise Fazenda, stopped the action to watch two half-starved kittens pawing at a loose board in the stage floor. Whispering down the chattering company he stopped and reached for one while the other let out a squeal and ducked back into the hole and oblivion. If that kitty had just let Eddie pick him up maybe his star would have risen as high as Pepper's.

While Eddie petted Pepper he instructed his cameraman to move in for a close-up. A property man quickly brought the ever present animal delicacies always on hand for such extemporaneous goings-on.

The business Cline thought up would have Louise spill some cream while pouring it into Sterling's coffee cup. The cream would drip down the leg of the table to the hole and then Pepper would crawl out and lick it up.

Eddie held Pepper with one hand, and dipping the finger of the other in the cream, let her lick it off. As if she had been acting all of her life he described what she was to do and then put her down in the hole.

Quietly he called for action, camera—the light was already on from the sun's rays which shone down from the roofless stage.

Slowly the cream dripped down and cautiously Pepper stuck first her paw up and then her head; and sniffing the cream, she dipped her pinky into a tiny rivulet, and with aplomb even a professional might not have had, with one take she completed the scene—to loud applause.

Mack Sennett constantly visited his various comedy companies. Sometimes he'd hide and watch the proceedings and then give his judgment; other times he'd just walk boldly onto the set and wait for his players to make him laugh. He was a wonderful audience and when King Mack laughed his thespians knew they had done some great clowning.

Mack's guffaw topped the applause and brought everyone to attention. Hiding behind a flat he had seen the whole kitty-kaper. Moving onto center-stage he squatted by the table and whispered as gently as a lover, "Here, kitty, here little puss, come to Papa."

Pepper stopped licking the cream on her paws. She peered at Mack with a dignity and poise that belied her age and disheveled appearance. And then, quite regally, she sidled over to him and crawled into his extended arms, and into such a lap of luxury as few kings could provide.

Giving her the once over, Mack suddenly made a proclamation, "From henceforth you shall be known as Pepper and I predict a long and brilliant career for another member of the Sennett realm."

Everyone applauded again and a property man brought forth a choice bit of catnip.

Pepper's fascination was in doing what other cat's didn't do. Startled, most felines flip their tails like a cop stopping traffic. Their ears fall back and their mouths become distorted into an ugly snarl. Not so Lady Pepper. She would quiver for a breathless moment and then look back quickly over her right shoulder—always her right shoulder. Her eyes enlarged to the size of quarters, their astonishment naive, the effect devastating. She would then tip her head to one side as if listening for the breeze to whisper a precious secret. When Mack saw this he said she was "as disarming as the lovely Lillian Gish."

Among a gallery of outstanding performances Pepper's emoting with the talented white mouse, Frederick Wilhelm, stood out. Dozens of cats before Pepper had tried and failed to complete a special sequence. For some unknown reason they wanted to make a meal of the mouse. One of the trainers quipped: "Maybe they've been fed on too much liver and cream and a little old mouse brings back fonder memories."

Pepper poses for the camera . . .

This special sequence was Pepper's first role as a Sennett regular. Could she curb her past savage urges? Eddie Cline and Mack watched with palpitations.

The scene opens with Mabel Normand setting down a bowl of milk for Pepper and the white mouse. They start lapping the milk and Mabel makes her exit. As the mouse gets a little over-anxious and his tail dips into the milk, Pepper stops lapping and looks at the rodent in elegant derision. A look that might kill, the audience thinks. But Pepper, being a lady, can't. She just raises her eyebrows, stiffens her whiskers and backs away from the dish. If there had been dialogue for the scene it would have been, "What poor manners!"

After the shot Sennett praised Pepper's performance and the new star nibbled on caviar. Was Pepper really that smart? Or had she had her fedupness of mice?

Mack Sennett's office was a building high above the grounds known as The Tower. Here heads and scripts rolled. Here the King could watch even a flea get out of line on one of his sets. In this atmosphere of friendly mayhem Mack had a Roman bath installed. While bathing, many of his funniest stories and plots were conjured up with a pack of gagsters hanging on every soap bubble. And here Pepper ruled beside her monarch. Many times Sennett turned to her as the final judge of an uncertain gag. As Pepper's whiskers would droop or stiffen so would the gag live or die.

In *The Kitchen Lady,* starring Louise Fazenda, Pepper stole the comedy chasing a canary. Louise tries to save the bird by climbing on the sink. The cat's tail falls into the basin where a black bass is swimming. The fish snaps at the cat's tail trying to pull him in the water. The cat leaps free and runs around in circles. A paper hanger is working in an adjoining room. The cat scrambles in the paste and wildly tries to shake it from its paws. The sequence was Sennett slapstick at its best.

During one conference Sennett came up with the idea of teaming Pepper and Teddy. The little cat and the big dog would be a natural for the gag-writers. The result was one of Keystone's funniest spine-ticklers.

There was never a show of temperament between Pepper and Teddy. Some felt not a little love passed between the Great Dane and the granddaughter of the *Felidae.* And the final fade-out for both was silent testimony to this supposition.

Teddy died at the age of twelve. The public was not informed because several films were scheduled and it was hoped one of his three sons might take his place.

. . . and plays with a friend, Wilhelm.

Everyone was fooled, everyone but Pepper. The first day on the set she looked at Caps, one of Teddy's offspring, raised her tail and spat and walked off the set. Not even King Mack, loaded with goodies, could find her as he searched the stages into the night.

When Pepper showed up a day later another son was tried out but his constant barking and wanting to play with her finished that hoax. She even refused to pose for publicity shots with a hidden leash holding Teddy's frisky son in tow.

"The Tower" swelled for a rocking conference. Pepper sat and watched, refusing to eat the finest of mouth-watering bribes. A half dozen vets examined her. She was perfect physically. The consensus —she was grieving for the departed Dane.

King Mack decided there was only one way out—to try a film with Pepper alone. He personally supervised every scene. But the public clamored for the famed team and something had gone out of Pepper's performing. She was not the same cat anymore. The King okayed a last try with the third son of Teddy.

That last day's shooting was not quickly forgotten by anyone in the fun factory. There was not a dry eye as Queen Pepper made feeble attempts at former greatness. She seemed to sense it—a farewell performance. As the dog and cat stumbled through the action King Mack stopped the camera and, picking up Pepper in his arms, ascended to "The Tower" with word he did not want to be disturbed by anyone.

No one really remembered what happened. But the next morning when the studio hummed with exploding autos and the splash of custard pies and the screams of chased heroines, Pepper was missing.

Search parties were headed by Mabel, Fatty Arbuckle and Mack. As the hours dragged by and Pepper was still missing the King called his funny subjects onto one of the stages. Making every effort not to be melodramatic, he said rather softly for even himself.

"Folks, I know you all loved her as much as I did. But she's gone. Of her own free will, I believe. Pepper came out of the blue to us and I think she's gone back to it."

The King blew his nose into a handkerchief.

"She had courage, that kitty. A lesson for all of us if a time like hers ever comes into our lives. She retired at the top. That's where her name will always shine. And I don't want no trainers hawking any other pussy around here! Pepper's our first and our last feline star!"

9 FOUR-LEGGED HAMLET

Newspaper reporters packed "The Tower," and photographers were all over the place. They were even standing in King Mack's massive tub. They were assembled for the signing of a contract that was unique in movie history. The name on the bottom line read "Teddy." He was a dog.

Keystone's publicity plutarchs posed Teddy, pen in paw, with Sennett looking over his shoulder. Teddy made his mark. The cameras clicked and the King had the top dog star in Hollywood for $40.00 a week.

A clause read:

"He, Teddy, shall render his services in a conscientious, artistic and efficient manner and to the best of his ability with regard to the careful, economic and efficient production of motion pictures and photoplays. It being understood that the production of motion pictures is a matter of art and taste."

Teddy was the screen's most versatile four-legger. Strongheart, Rin Tin Tin and Lassie, close on his heels, were strictly for drama while Teddy combined comedy with the drama. There really isn't much funny about a dog beyond his puppyhood. But when a dog acts like a man he's a riot.

Joe Simpkins guided Teddy's fabulous career with an iron hand. Not even King Mack directed him. Joe would talk over the scene with the director and then with Teddy, after which the big fellow would go through his paces like a veteran. He never missed a cue and his extraordinary memory put many a human co-star to shame.

How Joe discovered Teddy's talent was something he kept to himself. One day he brought the Dane to the fun factory and asked if they needed a big dog. Somebody said they did and when Teddy did a small bit in a Mabel Normand roughhouse the director called for King Mack, who promptly sensed a star had been born.

In one of his phenomenal routines, without a break in the action Teddy entered a kitchen door, which he had opened. He walked to the stove, lighted the fire with a match held in his teeth, moved to

Teddy "signs" contract for Mack Sennett.

the sink, filled the tea-kettle, went back to the stove, put the kettle
on the burner and then, taking up a broom, swept the floor.

To many Teddy was human and like a human he was temperamental. Not even Joe could handle him. For no reason he'd just
play "dead dog" on the set. At first everyone thought this cute and
humored him but when production stopped and nobody could rouse
the star, King Mack would be summoned.

After much coaxing and cajoling Sennett would tease him out of
his constitutional weakness. But the King's time was valuable and
he could only be in ten places at one time. But Teddy's tantrums
continued and in one of them Sennett was about to fire his great
star when Harry Langdon moseyed onto the set.

Baby-faced Harry almost dethroned Prince Charlie Chaplin with
his whimsical nonsense of getting in and out of trouble like a
grown-up baby. A long vaudeville career behind him, Harry played
every instrument in the jazz repertoire. As a hobby he collected
freak musical gear and his dressing room resembled a junk shop.

It was covered from floor to ceiling with every kind of music box, saw, banjoes made from cigar boxes, ukuleles from tin cans and a dozen or so harmonicas of all sizes.

Harry asked Sennett what was wrong with the Dane. "He's being human," snapped the King. Harry's mouth curled up in his face like the toes on an Oriental slipper. Whipping out a tiny harmonica, he said, "I'll get him on his feet quicker than you can say 23 skiddo!"

As "Turkey In the Straw" rollicked across the stage, Teddy's ears went up, his eyes popped, he looked at Harry, and before you could say 23 anything, he was prancing around the little comic like a cake-walker.

From then on Harry would be on call whenever Teddy kicked up his temperament. And when the lions or Anna May, the elephant, almost caught humanitis, Harry would cure them with his musical medication.

Teddy naturally had favorites among the dozens of top stars he played with. His dearest devotion focused on beloved Mabel Normand, whom many called a female Chaplin. Mabel was comparable to no one. She was Queen of silent comedy.

Duke, one of the zoo's ruling lions, was the only cat retriever of his day. He outdid the dogs in this difficult art. In Mabel's 1924 full length feature, *The Extra Girl*, Duke shared honors with Mabel and Teddy in one of the funniest gags to pop out of the Sennett jack-in-the-box.

The story in brief:

Mabel tries to break into movies as an actress, ending up working at every other job in the studio. The theme of the film was a warm and tongue-in-cheek spoof of early-day flickers.

In the scene with Teddy Mabel is a tailor's helper in the wardrobe department. She assists the cutter, Max Davidson, to fit a lion suit for Teddy, who is going to double for Duke, the real studio lion.

Mabel measures Teddy, tail and all. His tail doesn't want to be measured; it wags; it droops; it points like a pointer. She stops all this by placing the fake lion tail over Teddy's. Max watches in puzzlement. They put the lion suit on Teddy. Too big—the lion could get in with Teddy. Mabel plunges in with the scissors cutting every which way. Teddy, nipped a couple of times, endures silently. Mabel apologizes and then nips him again. Finally the repairs are finished and Mabel smiles in triumph. Teddy stalks around like a lion while Mabel, accidentally cutting off the tail, chases him to sew it back on.

This wonderful buffoonery is twofold. Later, when Mabel sees a lion come into the casting office where she is subbing for the telephone operator, she mistakes the real Duke for the doubling Teddy. Duke has escaped from his cage and has decided to prowl the lot.

When the telephone operator returns Mabel takes Duke and

Teddy with Mabel Normand and Max Davidson.

tieing a rope around his mane leads him all over the studio while everyone races for cover. Coming face to face with Teddy, out of the lion suit, Mabel takes a second look at Duke, realizing her predicament. But in the charming and naive way she was famous for she simply treats Duke like an overgrown pussy and leads him back to his cage.

Speaking of doubling, Teddy was the first animal star to merit a double. Performing a dangerous leap from a moving automobile onto a moving trolley car, Teddy slipped, breaking an ankle and almost losing his life. Sennett staged a never-to-be-forgotten tantrum and ordered his dog star not only to have a double for dangerous stunts but a stand-in for setting up the camera.

Not so Mabel Normand. She never had a double or a stand-in and she did stunts that sidelined many a professional, which sometimes included King Mack when he did an acting stint.

On working with animals and children the sage advice mumbled by W. C. Fields, a Sennett Alumnus, was classic, "Never work with kids and animals. They'll steal your best scene with their behinds to the camera."

Baby Boy John Henry, Jr. was a top offender in this category. He and Teddy teamed in some delightful one-reelers that ended up a draw as to who stole what. But the little boy and the big dog charmed film fans the world over as they recalled memories of their departed youth.

Teddy's star twinkled in the Hollywood skies for almost nine years. As well groomed as any Sennett luminary, male or female, he had his shampoos, massages, dental appointments, veterinary and chiropodist care at regular intervals.

On his fifth birthday the entire roster of Keystone comics chipped

Teddy enjoys attention lavished upon him by bathing beauty.

Teddy and son study poster of his latest film.

in and gave Teddy a new harness and a collar that cost over $100.

He was so loved by everyone that even when he wasn't before the cameras the other players asked for him to sit on the set just to pass on the scene. A yawn or a grin, or on rare occasions a bark, from the Great Dane was the highest compliment for such as Chester Conklin, Polly Moran or Vernon Dent.

"Now noiseless falls the foot of time . . ."

The shadow lengthened in Teddy's twelfth year. They cut his working day in half. For the first time he had retakes on his scenes. His courage and noble heart still brought laughs, but now misted with a tear.

One morning, doing a sequence with Pepper, Teddy collapsed and was rushed to the hospital. The Sennett foundry closed down for the day.

Several weeks later Teddy returned to the fold—as a spectator to watch one of his sons, Caps, make his debut under Del Lord's direction.

Well-wishers crowded around him and he cavorted a bit and did an added scene Del dreamed up.

As the final shot was taken, Teddy slowly looked around at all the familiar faces—Mabel, Fatty, Polly, Louise, Minta Durfee Arbuckle, Harry, and King Mack. Everyone said he smiled and then sagging a little walked up to his trainer. Joe had a hard time as he turned to the group, his hand on Teddy's jewelled collar: "Teddy is a little tired, but he wants to say goodbye folks and thanks for all the wonderful years. He'll be seeing you."

The shadows of the man and the dog crossed as they reached the car, and driving out of the gate a darker shadow fell on the pie-palace.

Three days later, Teddy died.

10 CONCENTRATING NUMA

Danger walks hand in hand with everyone on a lion movie. All the actors, crew, cameraman and director curtail any extra movement. It's as quiet as a tomb. And why? The slightest change in sound or position can put a jump that might prove fatal in a big cat.

The trainer stands behind the camera and catches the lion's eye. They stare at each other so intently an explosion seems the only outcome. But this concentration between man and beast is what builds up the trainer's control over the king of the jungle.

In the early days, lions let their eyes waver from the trainer and sometimes the crew were chased around for more than exercise.

Not so Numa. He surpassed all other cats in his extraordinary power to concentrate on his trainer. It was phenomenal to watch. Sometimes it seemed the man would jump on the lion and the lion on the man. They seemed one in this chain of eye-electricity. And when it all came out on the screen as Keystone belly-laughs it was even more phenomenal.

Madeline Hurlock was a voluptuous beauty Sennett somehow had sold on slapstick. Madeline could have been a vamp to rival Theda Bara. But the wild comical hysterics did something to her and playing straight to cross-eyed Ben Turpin, moustached Billy Bevan and the Keystone zoo flipped her.

Del Lord directed Madeline in many of these rollicking riots and their first time in a scene with Numa turned out to be quite a lesson for the experienced and sure-footed Mr. Lord and a proof of Numa's control.

Del explained that Madeline had to lie down on the floor and let Numa sniff her over and then put his paw on her chest. It seems she had fainted for some unknown reason and the lion was trying to revive her.

Dressed in a black satin, low cut evening gown with a rope of pearls around her neck and long earrings, Madeline gave Del the wide-eyed treatment.

Del fell in the woman-trap.

"Madeline, nothing to be scared about. Numa's just an over-

Mabel Normand and Numa in *The Extra Girl*.

grown pussy. He's been in pictures longer than any of us. Tame as a stuffed tabby. Look in his eyes. He's fallen for you already. Now, shall we shoot it, honey?"

Again Madeline's naive pretense deceived Del but no one else on the set.

"I believe you, Del, I believe every word. I don't exactly understand how you want me to play it. Shall I hold my breath? And what if Numa steps on my face? Shall I keep it straight?" Some giggles from the crew. Madeline trailed off as though she'd never been in a picture before. "You won't mind running through it for me, will you, Del? Once I see exactly what you want I'm sure we can do it in one take."

Del froze. He knew it. Madeline knew it. Everyone knew it. And King Mack hiding behind a set knew it and had to stick his fist in his mouth or burst out laughing. Del Lord, ace comedy director of madcap hilarity and Keystone murder was scared of Numa. Madeline had him dead to rights and only one way out—lie down and . . .

Del motioned to the trainer. Numa was brought into the set. Del started to lie down, he sort of broke in half, sitting first, knees up and then gradually slipping prone. He nodded to the trainer and Numa on signal moved into the set.

Numa's paws sounded like mild thunder on the stage. He towered over Del. He looked down at Del. He nuzzled Del's cheek. A kittenish snarl. The sweat rolled off Del's brow. And then Numa, like a king knighting one of his brave warriors, placed his paw on Del's chest knocking most of the breath out of him. But Del never made a move. As the trainer signalled Numa off the crew gave their director a hand.

As Del scrambled to his feet, dusting himself, regaining confidence and smirking a little at Madeline, she threw him a surprise good as a custard pie.

"Bravo, Del. I really didn't think you'd go through with it."

Del tried to look puzzled. "Now, Madeline, whatever's got into you?"

Slowly, sparks ignited in Madeline's eyes.

"You directors tell us actors to do anything that comes into your heads. Even if it's not in the script and you think it's funny. Anything for laughs. Who cares about bruises and broken bones? Well, this even things up a little. Too bad Numa didn't put a little more realism into his acting."

Taking her position on the floor she added a pinch of salt to her triumph.

"I never was afraid of lions. In fact I was born on a lion's rug in my mother's bedroom. You see, the ambulance was late!"

Vernon Dent and Duke eye each other warily in Sennett slapsticker.

11 JOSEPHINE—NO PART OF BONAPARTE

As the most photographed monkey in pioneer times, Josephine commanded the top salary of $25.00 a day. She never worked on contract. She never worked overtime. She never really worked. She loved mimicking human beings before the camera.

On the town one night Mabel and King Mack drove down Hollywood Boulevard. Mabel brought them to a screaming halt as she pointed across Mack's sight at a crowd on the corner. "Look, Moick," Mabel's favorite pronunciation. "Look at the darling little monkey."

Catching pennies and balancing them on her nose with Gabriel Gonzales, turning the crank on the hand-organ for background, Josephine was the cutest fur mite you'd ever lay eyes on.

Mack and Mabel played with Josephine for some time and when he handed her a five dollar bill and told her to report to work the next day, she pursed her lips into a delightful feminine "Oh" that was to be her trademark and key to fame.

Most monkeys when excited screw up their faces into grotesque masks. They also snarl thinking they can frighten away their fears, maybe. They also leap around turning their tails into pinwheels.

But not Josephine. She pursed up her lips in a funny little perk as though she was saying, "oh, oh, oh." It was devastating and though monkeys are fabulous imitators, no one on the Hollywood scene could find another monkey to "oh" like Josephine.

Her I.Q., some said, was above 140. Pretty high for even the film executives. She played golf. She played ball. She played pool. She drove anything on wheels.

Her wardrobe rivaled Gloria Swanson's. She either could play a glamorous lady or a tuxedoed gourmet. Her manners at table were the envy of every animal star.

Her high intelligence was best illustrated by a scene in a Sennett spill and pelt that could have meant disaster for her and the film makers.

In the scene she was supposed to carry a lighted stick of dynamite, real dynamite, across the roof where the villain tries to make his escape. The villain is supposed to dive into a chimney hoping to elude

50

her. She is to follow, and then drop the dynamite down on the villain—another booming ending to a Sennett hurricane.

But half way across the roof Josephine hesitated. She always liked to keep an eye on her trainer, Gabriel, who was not in sight this time. He was pitching pennies outside the stage.

A prop hand yelled at her. She backed up. The fuse was burning fast. The director shouted. Josephine searched the crowd for her Gabriel. There was only a sea of confused faces. The sea started to spread as the fuse burned shorter. Somebody yelled for Gabriel. As he rushed to the set he raised his hands for quiet and then spoke gently to Josephine.

"Don't listen to nobody but me, Josey. Sit down and figure it out. The stick in the hole. Figure it out for yourself. The stick in the hole. Like I do with my cigarette."

Gabriel took the cigarette out of his mouth, walked to a rubbish can and dropped it in.

Josephine stared at her master; at the dynamite; at the chimney. And suddenly the famous "oh" rounded out her lips and just as if it were a daily chore, she skipped over and dropped the about-to-blow dynamite down the chimney.

Bricks scattered like confetti! Josephine flew off the roof into her Gabriel's arms . . .

12 CLIFF-HANGING BONUS

"Minta, I'll give you a nice bonus if you'll hang onto that tree root and let Chester Conklin rescue you." This was Wilfred Lucas, one of Mack Sennett's directors, talking.

Minta Durfee Arbuckle looked down from the crest of the Pacific Palisades at Santa Monica, California, towering some three hundred feet above the highway and across to the endless Pacific Ocean stretching beyond the horizon.

In 1913 actors did crazy things. She must have been crazy to even think of taking her life in her hands for the five dollars she was being paid. But a bonus. . . She and Roscoe could use an extra dollar or two, since they had just started working in flickers.

She nodded and with a quick kiss from her young husband, crawled out on the root and began to dangle. As the camera ground she started screaming and kicking and Chester ran into the scene assuring her he would save her. In typical Conklin mayhem he almost sent them hurtling down the cliff, but he finally made the rescue.

Behind the camera Roscoe Arbuckle applauded and cheered the players. In the not too distant future the world would applaud him as the silent screen's funniest fat man.

Minta pulled herself back into shape on terra firma as Wilfred Lucas kissed her on the cheek and said, "Come over to my place tonight and pick up your bonus."

Heading home, Minta queried Roscoe. "What's he want me to pick up the bonus at his place for?"

"Probably a gag, darling. You know Wilfred—always one for pulling a gag."

That evening as they entered the Hollywood home of Lucas, he quickly motioned them to follow him into the kitchen, out into the yard, to the garage. Smilingly he pointed to an English pit bull mother and her five little pits rollicking on a blanket in a corner.

"What do you think of your bonus, Minta?" Lucas said as he held up a six-week-old male puppy.

The threat of rain had prompted Minta to carry an umbrella.

Roscoe Arbuckle and Luke in a Sennett comedy.

She half raised it as she remembered dangling three hundred feet for what she believed was a cash bonus. Roscoe sidled up to her.

"Honey," he pleaded, holding up another squirming male, "take this one." As the little fellow licked his cheek. "I know he's going to be the best pal we ever had."

The puppy chewed Minta's finger. And the love that bloomed

in an instant between humans and animal bound Minta, Roscoe and the little pit together.

"Wilfred, because this was all your doing and something I want to always remember, we'll call our 'bonus,' Luke."

And so the saga of Luke of the golden-tan (with four white feet and a white collar and a white streak between his big brown eyes) began with a cliff hanger and a raised umbrella.

As the movie careers of Minta and Roscoe lighted up the comedy skyline Luke shared in the spotlight. Roscoe and Luke were inseparable. When Roscoe started directing Mabel Normand and himself in some of the best Keystone laugh-getters, the dog was his shadow on the set.

One afternoon Roscoe was directed out of any funny business. He turned to Luke and said, "Luke, think of something funny." The little dog started chasing his tail. Mabel joined the act by letting Luke leap at one of her long black curls. Soon a cute scene followed and Roscoe put it in the film.

King Mack, seeing the rushes, asked who the dog was. Luke, sitting beside Roscoe, stood up and offered his paw to the mirth-monarch. And another star was added to the Sennett zoo.

When Sennett had a swimming pool built for his players Luke proved himself a water dog along with Roscoe and Mabel and Minta. For an extra thrill, divers would climb up a twenty-five foot ladder to a second springboard. One day Roscoe, on the top board, called for Luke to come up. Slowly the dog surveyed the ladder and then obeyed his master. He had never seen a ladder and yet he worked out how to climb it by himself. On the board he watched Roscoe make his big splash. In the pool Roscoe, with arms extended, called, "Come on boy, it's all right. You can do it, Luke. Jump, boy, jump!" And Luke did.

Luke's love of the water led to his saving the life of Minta's mother.

The Arbuckles had taken a house on the Santa Monica beach.

Luke, Arbuckle, and friends Buster Keaton and Al St. John.

Minta Durfee Arbuckle remembers happy days with her husband and Luke.

Morning and afternoon dips were the order of the day for everyone including Mrs. Durfee. One sunny morning Mrs. Durfee ventured a dip on her own. A big wave knocked her down and the undertow dragged her out to sea. Luke, inside the house watching from the window, burst through the back door, leaped a six foot fence and raced for the beach. Catching Mrs. Durfee by the bloomers he pulled her to safety. Minutes later a servant rushed to give her first aid.

As Luke nuzzled up to her, Mrs. Durfee, recuperating in bed with Roscoe and Minta watching, promised: "Luke, you shan't go unrewarded. From now on this precious pillow Minta bought for me shall be your very own."

Luke settled luxuriously on the Oriental cushion which had cost $150. What a life! A movie star and a hero all in one day.

Many amazing and amusing events marked the life of Luke but Minta recalled what she and Roscoe believed was tops for humor and human error.

"The scene opens on an animal shelter wagon parked on a corner down from the studio. Slowly the back doors are pushed open and two bear cubs scramble out. These were played by two of the smartest brownies I ever saw, Elsie and Nellie. They start down the sidewalk as Luke comes out of an alley. Seeing the cubs he takes after them; the cubs scamper down the street.

"Roscoe enters the scene arms loaded with groceries. As he sees the bears coming at him he drops the groceries and heads for a nearby telephone pole with the bears right after him. And not far behind is Luke.

"It was a scream to see two hundred and eighty pound Roscoe going up the pole with the little brownies on his heels. But the hysterics that weren't written into the script broke up everyone.

"Out of nowhere came sirens screaming, and the Edendale fire department—at the time an all-Negro unit—swung into view. Paying no attention to anyone, they hooked up their hose and started squirting the studio building in back of the pole where Roscoe was climbing. Roscoe, the bears and Luke, barking at the bottom of the pole, were all caught in the burst of water.

"Del Lord, trying to control his belly-laughs, finally shouted that the fire was down at Tom Mix's studio, not Sennett's. And without a word off they whizzed. We laughed ourselves sick. Later we found out there *was* a fire at Mix's and Del's gag saved one of the stages."

Luke lived to the ripe old age of thirteen. When Minta and Roscoe went their separate ways they shared him. He was the most traveled dog in America making dozens of trips from New England to California and back again.

When you visit Minta in her Los Angeles home the beautiful almost life-size color portrait of Roscoe and Luke greets you from the mantel.

And Minta seems to speak for them when she says:

"Love me, love my dog."

The grandfather's clock seems to tick louder for a moment.

"How I loved them both . . ."

13 WHAT IS BIGGER THAN AN ELEPHANT?

"What is bigger than an elephant? But this also is become man's plaything, and a spectacle at public solemnities; and it learns to skip, dance and kneel . . ."

Plutarch wrote that many centuries before Mack Sennett put a pachyderm named Anna May on his laughing film. She did all things Plutarch predicted and more: ballet routines; belly-flops to match Fatty Arbuckle's funniest; a walk some say Chaplin imitated. She sat up with the grace of a circus poodle and preened herself with her trunk like a peacock.

King Mack, who introduced the immortal Marie Dressler to the screen public in *Tillie's Punctured Romance,* once said, "Anna May's funnier than Marie and just as human." Of course he didn't say this to Miss Dressler.

Sennett always demanded iron-clad contracts from both human and animal actors. As with Teddy's signing he wanted Anna May's to be a highlight. It was—one he never forgot.

Under a huge tent on the lot outside the stages everything was festive, awaiting the big moment. The order of events—have Anna May dip her pinky in a tub of ink and place it on the massive contract-parchment Sennett had had the print shop make up.

Slowly Pat Lang, Anna May's trainer, led the gifted star to the table under the tent, gently explaining what was happening. Photographers swarmed around like bees. Reporters were busier. Sennett was beaming. Lang tapped Anna May's pinky and told her to dip it into the tub of ink. Her trunk, which some experts say is like a man's conscience, reached out wavering over the liquid stuff. Suddenly the wonderfully docile pachyderm squealed as though a pile driver had hit her. Rearing back on her hind legs she trumpeted to high heaven and then smashed the tub as all the spectators scattered.

Ten minutes later, as Lang had Anna May in tow at the exit gate, Sennett and company approached cautiously. Lang was grinning from ear to ear.

"Sorry, Mr. Sennett. *I* forgot. But an *elephant* never forgets."

King Mack was boiling. "What kind of joke is this? I couldn't

Charlie Chaplin stares in disbelief at Anna May in this scene from *City Lights*.

get those news hawks back here if I gave each of 'em a case of Scotch."

Anna May's trunk reached for the comedy King's shoulders; it seemed almost as if there were tears in her eyes.

Lang continued:

"As you know, Colonel Selig brought Anna May from India to perform in his zoo and act in pictures. She was only eighteen months old and I had to bottle-feed her. We treated her like the pinkish three foot baby she was. She had the run of the studio, making her first film with Kathlyn Williams in her 15 episode serial.

"Well, one day while exploring the lot she headed for the row of offices; finding a window open, she let her trunk in for inspection. Her squeals brought everyone to her side. As I tried to quiet her down I found myself covered in a blue liquid dripping from inside her trunk. One of the secretaries poked her head out of the office window and said her ink well was missing. It was in poor Anna May's trunk! How she wailed as I pulled it out. And washing that trunk was the hardest job I ever had. But the little thunderer's appreciation was so touching I soon forgot."

Anna May's trunk hung like a garland around Sennett's neck.

"You're so right, Anna May. An elephant never forgets. Us

humans could sure learn a lot from you pachys. Pat, how about you signing for the lady?"

This contract also had a curious clause which read:

"This property is not for sale and must be returned in as good condition as received, fair wear expected."

Colonel Selig had a sense of humor too.

Anna May was paid $125.00 a day and her trainer, $7.50.

Questioned by a rival producer about the high salary, King Mack quipped:

"I pay her by the pound. Maybe I should pay everybody by the pound, huh? Well, ten cents a pound for that kinda ham is cheap at any price, even if it isn't kosher."

During her teenaging at Selig's zoo Lang taught Anna May a charming act which she performed to the delight of audiences attending the animal shows.

Seated at a table she picked up a bell with her trunk and rang for the waiter, Pat, who brought her a tray of bananas. Finishing these off she rang again. Another tray of the yellowskins was brought in. She munched these down. Finally she moved over to a bed and lying down pulled the blanket over and in an hilarious business in which her trunk didn't want to go to sleep she pillowed it. Suddenly she sat up trumpeting in what appeared to be agonizing pain. Pat returned as the doctor. After examining her he scolded her that she was just faking, wanted attention. Pulling out a bamboo bottle

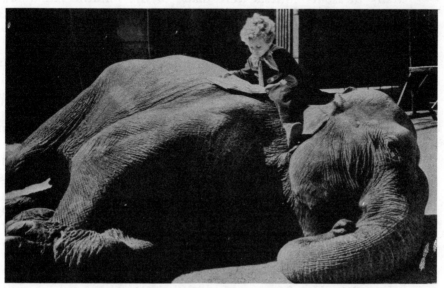

Anna May makes school days a little more pleasant.

Anna May training for her act.

of gruel from his black bag he put it in Anna May's mouth and she settled back, sucking contentedly.

Many unusual requests were made of the versatile Anna May during her long career that spanned both the silent and sound eras. But the day they asked her to be bigger topped them all.

How do you make an elephant bigger?

An Indian elephant by birth, she'd played the role of an African elephant by the simple use of some props. They just clamped a pair of big artificial ears and tusks over her smaller ones; on the Dark Continent tuskers grow taller and wider.

For the life of P. T. Barnum, *The Mighty Barnum,* many trumpeters tried out for the starring role of Jumbo. But none satisfied the producer and director. Someone suggested Anna May. Someone else said she wasn't big enough. But the call went out to at least interview her.

As Anna May and Lang waited on the stage some of the prop hands gave a few suggestions. But the producer and director were due in five minutes. How do you make an elephant bigger in five minutes?

A mattress was brought. Quickly they strapped it over her back and down her sides. How to hide it? Someone dug up a tent with black and white dots on it. Anna May watched the crew as if they were touched. But she loved any attention and if this brought laughs (making folks happy, that was her mission in life) she'd stand there all day. But why the padding in mid-summer? She never used a blanket even in the dead of winter.

As the producer and director entered the stage door, Lang whispered into Anna May's ear, "Take a deep breath, baby, and when they come up and look at you, expand like you never expanded."

"She's bigger than I remembered," the producer said.

Anna May expanded.

"She never looked that big when I used her in my last film," the director said.

Anna May, fully expanded, raised her trunk and trumpeted, shaking the stage from floor to rafters. She'd show them what a little sound could do—along with a mattress.

Anna May's behavior was established in many ways by the roles she played. No one had an explanation for this; it was just one of the eccentricities of being a pachyderm in pictures.

In *Hypnotized*, starring the Two Black Crows, she had a scene where she stole a plug of tobacco out of one of the boy's back pockets. After the take she ate the plug. And Lang recalled from then on she went "ape" for tobacco. She picked up every cigar and cigarette butt she found. Even a still smoking one never escaped her. She just put out the fire with her foot and then trunked it into her mouth. Quite a sight to see her steal a pack of cigarettes from an unsuspecting stagehand and crunch them down like they were peanuts.

A silly scene in a Keystone slapsticker with Mabel Normand got her on onions.

Mabel is peeling onions. The onions and tears get the best of Mabel and she leaves the kitchen. Anna May pokes her trunk through the window and sniffs the tear-jerkers. A close-up of Anna May devouring Spanish reds with tears streaming down her face almost stopped the camera.

Forever after Anna May demanded at least a dish of the *allium cepas* twice a week to satisfy her new craving.

Advertising a movie at Grauman's Egyptian Theatre she stopped traffic and the action by upsetting a vegetable wagon loaded with fresh green onions. No one was hurt and the publicity boosted the new film with headlines: "ANNA MAY RECOMMENDS NEW EGYPTIAN THEATRE EPIC BY CRYING ALL THE WAY THROUGH THE DRAMA . . ."

Anna May's credits were many but such films as *Tarzan of the Apes, Tarzan the Fearless, Tarzan and his Mate, The Lives of a Bengal Lancer,* and *Zoo in Budapest,* stand out for the most loved and talented tusker in the cinema jungle.

Since Pat Lang was both trainer and foster-father to Anna May, he best explained the events underlying her inspirational and heart-warming saga.

"People often ask me what I do to prepare Anna for a scene when we are working in pictures. If she is to walk from here to that tree, stop, trumpet, and then pick up the man lying on the ground, I rehearse her a couple of times. I walk alongside her and show her just what I want her to do, let her do it once or twice, and then when the cameras are ready she will go right through with the same action.

"If the sound apparatus is not on, I can call to her. They sometimes take a silent shot and put the sound in later. They often have to shoot a scene two or three times before they are satisfied with it, but Anna will work as long as we want her to.

"I know a lot about elephants but a person could never learn all there is to know. I have worked with them for thirty-seven years and have broken one hundred and thirty-one, but there is always something new to learn. A day never passes that Anna doesn't do something new, some little thing I have never before seen her do. Elephants are like monkeys that way—always up to new tricks. Anna has been unusually successful in pictures because she is very intelligent, has a fine disposition, remembers what I teach her and works willingly.

"I have known close to five hundred elephants in my day and Anna beats them all."

The comedy villain was rare in films. It was difficult to be mean and funny. Vernon Dent was both and yet liked by fans though he harassed the film antics of such loveables as Harry Langdon, Charlie Chase, the Three Stooges and dozens of other comics.

Cutting his celluloid teeth on animals and custard pies at the Keystone Kapery, Vernon fell in love with Anna May the first day he and Harry Langdon played a scene with her.

"She was incredible. She was human, like Sennett said. And she loved the camera. The minute it clicked you could see a change come over her.

"I shall never forget a day in which that same click almost turned her into a killer.

"The picture was called, *Soul of the Beast,* starring beautiful Madge Bellamy. It had a circus background, and this time I played a real mean villain.

"A small one-ring circus the scene. Madge is found lying unconscious in the sawdust by Anna May, who, thinking she is ill, kneels over her body and caresses her with her trunk.

"They rehearsed it twice and the director said, 'Camera! Action!'

"Anna May moved into the set. A substitute trainer had been assigned to her. And since she always took direction from the trainer, she never obeyed any other signal from behind the tripod.

"As the action progressed, for some unknown reason, the trainer signaled Anna May to lie down—lie down on Madge!

"She started to lie down instead of kneel and then suddenly she sensed something was wrong as she saw the terror in Madge's eyes. The trainer tried another signal. Anna May, now confused, swayed back and forth as we all watched in horror.

"She blinked at the trainer who now had the windup. He still gave the wrong signal. She squealed and trumpeted. Again a bewildered look at the trainer. We all knew there was nothing anyone else could do. We just had to wait and pray.

"Slowly Anna May let her two-ton body down on Madge. Madge fainted. Behind the camera Madge's mother fainted. Anna May's massive hulk was inches away from the unconscious girl. And then as if she realized what the danger was, she extended her trunk between her own body and Madge's, and wrapping it around her pulled her to one side and then dropped on both knees, thundering up sawdust clouds.

"It was the most fantastic ad lib performance by any animal in films. And the cameraman—frozen with fear—had stopped turning the crank. He also had fainted."

Is there anything bigger than an elephant?

Yes, Mr. Plutarch—his heart.

14 CANINE MOVIE FANS—1915 VINTAGE

I have often wondered how the animals outside the movie realm felt about their brothers appearing before the magic lantern. Do they envy them? Do they long as humans long for the glamor and fame that set them apart from the rest of humanity?

A very curious and original thinking writer by the name of Ernest E. Dench did some world-wide researching and in an article published in the July, 1915 issue of *Photoplay Magazine,* following dozens of interviews with dog owners around the globe, came up with the following facts.

A friend of mine in London has a dog who always follows her when she goes to the movies. He isn't content with sitting in her lap, but always takes good care to use a whole chair for himself. His way of applauding a film is to wag his tail against the metal back of the chair, and if he does not like the picture he is bad-mannered enough to turn his back on the screen. He reminds his mistress when the program has been given the once over by tapping her with his paw.

Up in Scotland I once heard of a Glasgow fan who has a bow-wow of the canine variety. Once she took him to see the movies and the dog was so befogged by his strange surroundings that he went to sleep in the arms of his mistress. After a number of these visits he began to sit up and take notice. Strong drama causes him to bark loudly, while when a comedy comes on the screen he pricks up his ears. I am not going to try and make you believe he laughs, but my own small opinion is that it is the canine way of expressing the emotion.

An American fan, on seating himself to enjoy a photoplay performance, had an unwelcome visitor in his dog, who had entered without paying. At first he behaved himself like a gentleman, but when a hold-up appeared in a Western drama, he barked and then attacked the screen as if to attack the wrongdoers. Fortunately, however, the operator had viewed the incident through his peep-hole and had sufficient presence of mind to turn on the lights. This saved the situation, for the dog hastily retired when the film disappeared, and looked at the screen with a puzzled stare. He then walked back meekly to his master.

Sometime ago a building contractor residing at Lakewood, New Jersey, took his dog to a local photoplay theatre. The canine became such an ardent moviefan that he ambled in the show for forty days in succession without his master's authority. How the man discovered this was by receiving a bill for four dollars, specifying the number of visits the dog had made. The artful exhibitor had decided to turn the canine's infatuation to profitable account. And who could blame him?

The unintentional victim refused to pay the amount, and when sued in the county stated that his mongrel had no business to be permitted to enter unless he had a ticket. The court ruled in his favor.

Going further afield—India, to wit—a motion picture exhibitor related to me an incident which occurred at his theatre. This took place when he put on a film entitled, "The Police Dogs of Paris," revealing a bunch of these intelligent creatures pursuing some Apaches.

A stray dog somehow managed to wriggle into the show unseen when this picture was being shown and the police dogs struck him as being so real that he made a dive for the screen, barking furiously all the time. Just as he reached the screen an Apache shot at the dogs and the audience was astounded to see the real dog fall down helplessly.

The real explanation was that the dog, on butting into the wall of the building, had been momentarily stunned. He soon revived, however, and his many howls gave evidence that he resented his defeat, after which he made his getaway.

A personal footnote to canine fans.

Whenever I attend a drive-in movie my mixed Beagle, Chou-Chou, many times accompanies me. She watches the film attentively with one or two naps. But I honestly don't know whether she's a dyed-in-the-wool movieite or not. The minute the lights go up and the intermission is on she starts barking and leaping for that pizza pie at the snack-bar.

15 A DOG'S LIFE

Brownie, the bull fox terrier, was the only actor besides little Jackie Coogan to steal a film from Charlie Chaplin. Jackie did it in *The Kid,* and Brownie did it in, *A Dog's Life.*

Charles Gee on a rainy afternoon cut through an orange grove near Hollywood and Vine and came upon a man wrestling with a small white dog. In trying to chain him, the chain had struck the animal several times, drawing blood. Gee leaped at the fellow, raising his fist for a haymaker.

The man frantically explained he was the city dog-catcher. A lady had reported the dog overturning garbage cans and making a nuisance of himself. He was only doing his duty.

The frustrated fur bundle huddled at Gee's feet, his eyes pleading for protection, someone to love; right there he found his object. Gee handed the dog-catcher a couple of bills and said he'd take care of the dog. As the man retreated Gee picked up the tousled pooch and was immediately wet-cheeked with kisses.

As he walked out of the sweet-smelling grove, he wondered what to call the canine.

The animal's blue eyes stared at him; one eye had a brown patch which spread to his ear.

" 'Brownie,' how's that? Can't mistake you for Brownie, can they? You like the name?"

The tail wig-wagged wildly and the kisses were applied like a paint brush.

Gee began training Brownie just for the fun of it. The dog would obey any command and enjoyed doing anything his master asked. Neighbors and friends were amazed at his behavior. Gee took him everywhere and he was better behaved than any seven year old.

About this time (1918) Charlie Chaplin was preparing *A Dog's Life,* a comedy-drama featuring a tramp and a stray dog and drawing satiric and pathetic comparison between them.

Dozens of dogs paraded in front of the baggy-pants comic. But none measured up to his imaginary canine character whom he called Scraps in the flicker.

Edna Purviance, Brownie, and Charlie all agree it's *A Dog's Life*.

A friend read about Chaplin's difficulties in the paper and suggested Gee take Brownie for an interview. Just for a lark Gee telephoned the casting office and was promptly given an appointment.

Brownie sensed the moment. How, not even Gee knew. As he followed his master onto the street-scene where Chaplin was working he took on the most woebegone, forlorn look any four-legger ever endured. Approaching Chaplin, who was wearing his tramp outfit with his shoes on backward and his clothes looking like they'd belonged to three different men, he recognized a fellow traveler. For an electric second the dog stared at the silent screen's greatest clown and then slowly he leveled himself to his belly and just looked as sad as any mongrel can at the saddest eyes any clown had ever circled with greasepaint.

"What's his name?"

Gee whispered it.

"Well, Brownie, how'd you like to be a movie star?"

The dog jumped on his lap, washing his face with kisses. Delighted, Chaplin returned a few. Another dog-star took its place in the cinema firmament.

Scenes like the following, from *A Dog's Life,* show the little film as a small masterpiece and its players as geniuses.

The first scene discovers the tramp asleep by a fence in a vacant lot with Scraps snoozing in a basket by an ashcan. The cold wind forces the tramp to stuff up a draft from a knothole with his tattered handkerchief.

Later Scraps finds some food in the street. Other dogs rush in to grab it. Scraps tries to fight them off. The tramp comes to his aid by lifting him high above the leaping, barking melee. As the tramp skips down the street one of the dogs hanging to the seat of his pants rips a hole in them.

A milk bottle resting on a doorstep tempts Scraps. Unable to lap out the milk the tramp comes to Scrap's aid by sticking the dog's tail in the bottle. He proceeds to lick it off.

At a food stand selling cakes and sausages, the tramp converses with the proprietor while Scraps swipes a string of weiners. When the owner turns his back the tramp wolfs down the cakes. The owner's suspicions mount; the tramp pretends he's shooing flies from the cakes. A cop comes up and Scraps and tramp duck as the tramp slaps the cop with a big wurst.

That night the tramp seeks shelter in the Green Lantern Café. Hiding Scraps in his oversize pants, he threads his way through wildly dancing couples, the dog's tail wagging out of the hole in his trousers. As the couples hem the tramp in near the orchestra, Scraps's tail beats the drum—to the bewilderment of the drummer.

Later, in the vacant lot, Scraps, foraging for food, digs up a thick wallet some crooks had buried after rolling a rich man. With money to burn, the tramp and Scraps return to the café. Edna, a simple country girl, is making her singing debut. She and the tramp fall in love at first sight.

Crooks recognize the wallet in tramp's hand and roll him. But all ends well as Scraps gets wallet and police get crooks. For a heart-warming ending, the camera tilts from a smiling and kissing Charlie and Edna to Scraps and a litter of puppies of which he is the proud father.

Brownie's almost human performance prompted Julie and Abe Stern to sign him up for five years during which he starred in 50 two-reelers.

Brownie was also a star-maker. Baby Peggy Montgomery played in one of his flickers, *Pals.* She was a delight and a hit. This led to a series. Following this Baby Peggy starred in such features as *Captain January* and *The Law Forbids.* She opened the camera lens to Shirley Temple.

Unlike his human co-workers, Brownie didn't have a jealous bone in his body. He loved playing with other animals and one of his favorites was Queenie, the trick horse known as the Royal Lady of filmland's equine set. Queenie and Brownie saved children from burning buildings, rescued maidens locked in barns and dragged wounded heroes to safety.

Brownie's story was in the true tradition of rags to riches. Yet his stardom and fame never swelled his head. To his last breath he loved and obeyed master Gee's every command. Some say animals don't remember. Brownie remembered that rainy afternoon in the orange grove to the end of his life.

16 A THOUSAND POUNDS OF DYNAMITE

William S. Hart rode him up and down the Hollywood rainbow trails from 1915 to 1925. Weighing only a thousand pounds his power and endurance outdistanced any other horse twice his weight.

With Cactus Kate he rocked cinemaland in one of its most sensational four-legged romances. Caught in a whirlpool for a dangerous sequence, he and his master prayed for help to save their lives.

His name was Fritz and not even Tom Mix's Tony could outshine his western star.

Fritz loved to stunt on or off camera. When Harry Aitken, President of the Triangle Film Corporation, told Bill he had brought out a party of ladies to his camp to see him, Bill decided to give the feminine contingent a thrill to remember.

As the ladies huddled in a talkative group, Bill asked them not to move; he was going to show them one of Fritz's outstanding feats. Riding the paint pony about two hundred yards distant, then whirling and galloping at full speed, he headed Fritz toward the group. As startled mouths started to scream, Bill threw Fritz right at their feet without kicking up a shoe full of dust. Bill's head grazed one of the dowagers on the ankle. Catching their breaths they applauded and all agreed it was the biggest moment in their lives.

This was a dangerous stunt. There was a 90 per cent chance that either man or horse would be injured, because Fritz's weight hit on his left shoulder when he fell. But Bill had thrown his package of horse-dynamite in dozens of westerns, and neither had ever suffered serious injury.

Fritz had a sense of humor. And so did Bill Hart. It was a question as to who out-sensed the other. Sometimes Bill had to leave Fritz in a barn on Washington Boulevard in Los Angeles. When Bill showed up anything could happen.

The little pinto loved his master but he just didn't like being left alone for any length of time. Following one of Bill's absences, Fritz decided not to make up with Bill. Bill tried coaxing him with a tidbit. As Fritz reached for it Bill vaulted into the saddle. Fritz blew his stack and almost bucked Bill onto Washington Boulevard.

But any rider could stay on the pony because he didn't weave, sunfish or spin, just bucked straightaway.

Fritz never had a double. In *Truthful Tulliver,* made in 1916, Bill rode Fritz smack through a plate glass window and neither of them even got scratched.

Bill realized that if any other horse took his place it would crush the pony. He loved to act and he loved his master. But due to a temporary layoff, Fritz had to endure another horse, Jack by name, working in a rescue scene with Bill. It was an almost fatal experience for the leather-skinned western hero.

The scene had Bill riding up a steep bank with a fence on one side. For some unknown reason Jack wouldn't do the ride so a handsome three year old black stallion was doubled.

But as Bill mounted the stallion he bucked furiously and up the bank they leaped. The saddle horn had hit Bill in the stomach and he almost passed out from the terrific impact. But he hung on as the wild black bucked and bucked, scraping against the wire fence and then lurching toward the bank. Regaining his senses while everyone else stood by helplessly, Bill sunk the iron deep in the black's sides. He scrambled up the bank to safety.

William S. Hart and Fritz in *Pinto Ben*.

Later when Fritz had recovered and he and Bill were waiting for a scene to be set up, the pony nosed Bill's stomach. Under his shirt a large bruise still hurt. He had it for months. But how did Fritz know about it? He did, because he looked up at his master and almost said, "wouldn't have happened if you'd been on me, Bill."

Bill decided to top all other equine stunts with his pinto pony. Galloping along the edge of a cliff Fritz would be shot by an escaping bandit. Fritz and he would roll to the gorge below. The first drop would be about 12 feet, followed by a stretch of over a hundred. Bill knew they could do it.

But Cliff Smith, the director, shook his head. It wasn't worth it to dare fate with such a valuable property. Everyone agreed and finally Bill listened to Smith's substitution for the hair-raising action.

A dummy horse that looked exactly like Fritz was built at a cost of over $2,000. The scene was shot like this. Hart raced Fritz and then threw him. The dummy was doubled and held by piano wires as Bill mounted it. The camera ground, the wires cut and down Bill and the dummy plunged to the gorge. The illusion was perfect as the real Fritz and the dummy shots were matched.

So Fritz *was* doubled once and Bill Hart faced a peck of trouble from the New York City censors following the premiere of the picture. The censors believed Fritz had been exposed to possible injury and maybe death for the fantastic sequence.

Only one way to prove the censors wrong—go to New York and run the film. This Bill did showing how the fake was made and the illusion accomplished. The censors apologized and praised the amazing camera magic.

But the public always believed Fritz and Bill tumbled down that cliff together and thousands of letters bore testimony to their faith that the incomparable pair could defy even death.

The turbulent romances behind the scenes in cinemaland have many times been more dramatic and headline-making than some of the hit screen scenarios: Mary Pickford and Douglas Fairbanks; Vilma Banky and Rod La Rocque; Greta Garbo and John Gilbert.

But none of these off-camera lovers created the sensation wildfired by Fritz and Cactus Kate. Riding down to jaw with friends working with the 101 Show of Cowboys and Indians, which was rehearsing in the Santa Monica Canyon, Bill and Fritz enjoyed even the landsacape over which they had kicked up the sod in so many shoot-em-uppers.

Between watching the rehearsals and Bill's shop-talk with the Indians and riders, Fritz wandered off. This was the pinto's habit. He never ran away. He just liked to do a little nosing on his own. But this was a nosing to make Jimmy Durante's look like a minnow's.

Sometime later Hart, looking for Fritz, found him mooning over

Bill Hart and Fritz in *The Narrow Trail*.

a mule mare used in the covered wagon routine. Hart tried to mount Fritz, but the horse shied away, almost throwing him. A crowd gathered. Fritz turned his tail to Bill, as he ogled Cactus Kate as if she were the most beautiful creature on four legs.

With every nuance known to a horseman, Bill Hart eventually mounted Fritz and rode away, leaving Cactus Kate dewy-eyed in the sunset.

As he bedded down for the night William S. Hart, who had faced crises both off and on film, wondered about his pinto pony and his lady friend.

When Bill opened the corral the next morning Fritz lay on his side staring at the ceiling. Bill called a vet. After examination he told Bill the little horse was the strongest critter he'd seen in a long time. What was wrong? Heart trouble, the vet quipped. Hart's blood-pressure rose as he felt the vet pulling his leg. The vet grinned. Not the organic, the romantic. Fritz was in love. Bill's usually thin slit eyes burst open like acorns. Cactus Kate! That mule femme fatale. Guess, only one thing to do.

"Well, Fritz, how about a canter out to the 101 Show?"

The pony rose to his feet like he'd been battery-charged.

Spying Cactus Kate hitched to a wagon Fritz galloped up and practically fell on his knees in front of her while Bill straddled him red-faced as a berry. As the cowpokes and injuns gathered 'he just kept up making palpitating love to the mule mare. The roars of laughter drowned out the Pacific ocean below. And William S. Hart just had to sit and watch with his neck nearly on fire with embarrassment.

After friendly bargaining, Bill bought Cactus Kate and as they headed for home with Kate loping alongside like a blushing bride he recalled she was an "outlaw," who wasn't good for anything but bucking in the Show's program. Sighing heavily he hoped she wouldn't buck Fritz out of his star-rating.

But on the next location scenes in Victorville, California, another Kate crisis arose. Kate stayed at home while Fritz acted in the little desert community. But Fritz didn't act. He acted up. He fought, bucked and reared. Even ran off. After several hours of this cutting-up Bill realized it was Kate again so a truck was sent hurry-up to fetch her and quiet the temperamental star.

At sight of Kate little old Fritz performed as never before. It was incredible and nerve-wracking. What did this Kate dame have after all? As they rubbed noses Bill Hart surmised that horses were far from being human in the way they chose their mates.

On location in Sonora, Tuolumne County, California, for the 1920 thriller *The Toll Gate*, the little pinto horse and the man of steel almost lost their lives.

In his book, *My Life East and West*, William S. Hart described this harrowing experience as no one else would dare.

About sixteen miles from Sonora we found a swift-running stream which tunneled right through a mountain. It was the most wonderful place in the world for an entrance to our bandit cave. The tunnel was about one hundred yards long. At the entrance there was an overhanging ledge which made a roomy cavern. At the back of the cavern was the round hole through the mountain, varying in size so little that it might have been the handiwork of man, but it was made by nature, and in it my little friend and I shook hands with death.

Lambert, my director, and Joe, the camera man, and their assistants, had looked over the place the day before. Joe had stripped and followed the swift stream through the mountain on a raft, sounding for depth with a long pole. He reported about eight feet of water, except in one strip some thirty feet long where he could not touch bottom. There was some six feet of width on the water-line, and the arched roof was about the same distance in height at the center. The camera men were to place their cameras at the upstream end of the tunnel where we were to come out, and we were to swim against the current and carry heavy torches to give them sufficient light to photograph us as we made the trip.

There were nine of us to go through, single file, eight feet

Bill Hart and Fritz pose in a desert setting.

apart. There wasn't any talking—we all realized that it was a mighty serious piece of business. I told the boys, as we loosened our cinches, that any one who wanted to draw out could do so. No one did.

I was to go first. The second man was not to follow until I had gotten across the strip where Joe had not been able to find bottom. I am positive that this decision saved the lives of at least two horses and two men. The thirty-foot strip was a bottomless whirlpool or well. Once an animal got into it, he could neither swim nor climb out. There was no bottom for his hind legs to reach and he could only get his front hoofs on the ledge which was six feet under water.

Almighty God! How Fritz did try! He struggled. He screamed. He looked at me with the eyes of a human being. He actually climbed the arched side walls until he turned himself over backwards. Twice we went down in those cold, whirling depths and twice we fought our way to the surface again. I knew the next time would be the last. Fritz spoke to me—I know he did. I heard him, and I spoke to him. I said, "God help us, Fritz" . . . and God did help us!

My little friend could not struggle any more, his eyes were glazed with coming death, as we were going down for the last time the strong current we had been fighting carried us over the ledge back toward the way we came in, and as we sank we touched bottom and regained our feet.

We were saved! God saved us! I know He did, and I know my little horse knew He did, because when we came out we sank down on our knees and said a little prayer before the sun stopped shinin' an' we were asleep. . . .

On September 20, 1958, the William S. Hart Park in Newhall, California, better known as "Horseshoe Ranch," was dedicated and opened to the public. Here the great western star had spent many happy years and because he wanted to perpetuate the real "spirit of the west," he collected many relics from that past and willed the ranch to the County of Los Angeles.

A stone's throw from the corral and barns is the last resting place of a thousand pounds of dynamite—Fritz. Above the grave rises a bronze marker inscribed—"To Bill Hart's Pinto Pony Fritz, Age 31 Years. A loyal Comrade . . ."

17 SUPPORTING PLAYERS

To most of the motion picture public during the early silent days, Mary Pickford was the morning star in its heavens. As the first star her acting triumphs as "America's sweetheart" were legendary.

Mary's cooperation and friendliness with her fellow players were also legend until she starred in a 1919 film, *The Hoodlum*. Sidney Franklin directed, and Kenneth Harlan was her leading man. My mother did a bit role in the sequence where Mary, for the first time in her golden-curled career, refused to work with some supporting players and threatened to walk off the set.

But Mary's blowup set the fuse that sky-rocketed this group to a rare but hardly enviable stardom: the most loathed and yet most celebrated of their kind in flickerville. But following the Pickford near scandal the demand for their services bordered on the fantastic.

It all started with Sidney Franklin quietly giving last-minute instructions to Miss Pickford and company.

"Now that I've explained the action and business I'd like you to think about the mood. Mrs. Lee is seriously ill with consumption. Her children are playing in the streets, hungry, without proper clothing, unattended. Mary you're frightened by the drab surroundings but try not to show it as you enter the room. Any questions?"

Franklin lit a cigarette and walked over to a man who was standing behind the bed that my mother lay on.

"Everything in order, Mr. Turner?"

Mr. Turner nodded.

Franklin turned to the rest of the company.

"Places everyone." He leaned over my mother and said, "Mrs. Lee, don't forget to cough when Miss Pickford and Mr. Harlan enter." Franklin sat in his director's chair beside the camera. There was a moment of silence. Quietly he said, "Lights. Camera. Action."

Mary and Harlan entered. Mary was carrying a basket of fruit. Harlan was holding a bundle of clothes. Mary crossed to the bed and sat beside my mother, smiling.

About to speak, she suddenly jumped up screaming, backing into Harlan, scattering the bundle of clothes all over the set.

"Bed bugs! Bed bugs! Sidney, bed bugs are crawling all over that wall behind Mrs. Lee. Awful bed bugs!"

Franklin caught her in his arms. Her golden curls fell in his face like a rag-mop.

"Now, Mary, steady yourself. They aren't real bed bugs."

Mary stamped her foot, shaking her curls that now looked like the million dollars they were worth.

"What do you mean they aren't real bed bugs? I've seen bed bugs for real more times than I care to remember, and those bugs are the realest I've ever seen. Oh, I'm itching all over!"

Franklin said, "I didn't mean they aren't real bed bugs, they are but ——"

"No buts about it, Sidney. Get them out of here before we're all eaten alive!"

Mary picked up her fur coat from a chair.

"Those bugs won't bite, Mary. I promise everyone in the company no harm will come to them."

"Sidney, you'll have to excuse me for the day. And you'll have this stage fumigated before I work on it again!"

Franklin grabbed her gently by the shoulders as she moved toward the exit.

"Mary, calm down and please listen to me while I explain."

"What's to explain? Those bugs will have multiplied ten times while we're standing here talking."

"Mary, those bed bugs are actors."

Mary choked on a laugh.

"Actors? Sidney, you're joking." She stared into his steady blue eyes. "No, you *are* serious. Very well, Sidney, explain away."

Franklin smoothed his moustache.

"That man standing over there is Mr. Turner. He specializes in insect and animal oddities for pictures. He's the bed bugs' trainer and manager. He guarantees his bugs won't bite—in writing."

Mary paced back and forth.

"I've done everything possible and sometimes impossible for the past ten years in motion pictures, but I simply refuse to work with bed bugs, trained or not!"

"But, Mary, it's only for the picture's sake. Think of the terrific impact on the audience when I show you and the bed bugs in a close-up."

"I can see the newspaper headlines now: MOVIE HOUSE EMPTIED BY PICKFORD BED BUGS! No, Sidney, I refuse!"

Franklin caught an arm of her fur coat as she reached the exit.

"Mary, we are pioneers in a new art form. The screen needs realism now. What an opportunity! How can its greatest star stand in the way of progress?"

You could hear a bed bug talk.

"Sidney, you know, I have never refused anything my directors have asked." Slowly moving back to the set. "I won't begin with you." Her fur coat dropped in her chair. "I'll play with these trained dots on the wall. But on one condition—no close-up with me and those bed bugs!"

18 THE BIGGEST THREE

In 1917 directors Sidney and Chester Franklin formed the Fox Kiddie Company of juveniles ranging from seven to ten years and playing grown-up parts in such classics as *Jack and the Beanstalk, Aladdin and His Lamp* and *Treasure Island.*

But my greatest thrill, and disappointment, came the day we began work on *Six Shooter Andy* starring the biggest three on the western panorama—Tom Mix, Tony, the wonder horse, and Duke, the Great Dane, with the Franklins directing.

My uncle, Hank Potts, a pioneer stunt and trick horseman was also on the picture and during a lull in the action he asked me how things were going.

"Well, this being our first day, us Fox Kiddies expected something really terrific to happen."

"Like what?"

"Like something the most terrific cowboy in the world would do."

"So?"

"So Tom rides on the set in a big shiny car with Tony behind in a trailer and Duke sitting in the front seat."

"Now, Ray, don't let that take any of the kick out of you. Tom drives his cars like his nags. Tom's all and more than's ever been said or written about him. Did you know he was once a Texas Ranger?"

"A Texas Ranger?"

"Right. And he was also a Rough Rider under Teddy Roosevelt and a volunteer in the Philippine uprisings. He also saw military service in the Orient during the Boxer Rebellion and was a Range Rider in El Paso."

"Wait 'til I tell the other kids!"

My uncle handed me a piece of chewing gum and popped one in his mouth himself and we both started chewing hard as he really shook me up with a story that had never been told.

"You wanta hear a horse story to end all horse stories?"

I nodded because I couldn't wag my tongue.

Tom Mix and Tony pose in this scene from *Soft Boiled.*

"It's hard to believe, but I once bought and sold a million dollar property and lost fifty cents on the deal."

Uncle Hank popped his gum and I tried but failed. I never could pop gum.

"Pat Crissman—Tom's manager—and me have been good friends since I first rode into pictures as a punk kid. Always looking around for a bargain in horse-flesh, we wandered down to Fifth and Central in L.A. to an auction. There weren't any bargains but not wanting to come back empty-handed we bought a sorrel pony for $12.50. Pat had only six bucks so I put up the rest. I worked and tried to train the horse but he didn't show anything at all."

"But Uncle Hank, with all the horses you've trained and ridden how could you make such a mistake?"

He shook his head and popped his gum.

"Well, to get on with the story, sometime later Tom's great horse, Blue, died. Tom was really busted up. He loved that horse like you would your best friend. Meeting Pat Crissman in Fat Jones's barn one day, Pat said he had to do something about Tom's moping. It seems he couldn't find a horse for Tom and things were getting serious with a heavy schedule of films coming up."

I interrupted.

"And he wanted you to sell your interest in the sorrel pony so he could give him to Tom?"

"How'd you guess? Well, I said sure. I didn't think the nag would amount to much. Maybe be a horse-double. Nothing else. Again Pat had only six bucks. But I took it thinking I was well out of losing just six bits."

My uncle was a little man, taped with TNT, who could ride anything on legs. He looked even smaller as he concluded a tale even the *Arabian Nights* couldn't top.

"Pat Crissman gave the pony to Tom. It was love at first sight. And now looking over at the sorrel I wonder if I ever had a brain in my head. Yes, he turned out to be Tony that million dollar pony you saw riding in the trailer this morning, dear nephew!"

The exploits of Tom and Tony were legendary and the bond between them as inspiring as their fame. Two near fatal accidents prove the love that bound them together in every riding moment.

On May 5, 1915, Tom Mix rode in a rodeo at the Los Angeles Stadium. Tom, on Tony as an outrider, galloped neck and neck in the chuck wagon race with two four-horse wagons. Suddenly the teams collided. Curly Eagles, driving close, leaving just enough room for a wagon to pass, tried to motion Tom not to close on him. At this instant a bridle strap broke on Eagles's leaders. There was a grinding crash and Eagles and Mix literally mixed it up, spilling Tony, pinning both against the rail. Tom and Curly were rushed unconscious from the scene. Tom suffered a broken jaw, crushed chest, fractured leg and dangerous internal injuries. Tony was miraculously unhurt.

For a week Tom Mix fought for his life.

During this crisis Tony refused to eat. He lunged at the groom who tried to enter his stall. Once a day he would take a little water.

When Tom regained consciousness and asked about Tony and was told of his behavior he demanded to be taken home. The reunion of man and horse was a tear-jerker even for the most saddle-skinned. Hand-fed by his master, Tony began eating again.

Years later in the Santa Cruz mountains of the Golden State, the script called for Tom and Tony to chase a pack of villains along a narrow trail flanked by overshadowing mountains. The villains had planted dynamite on the trail which, as Tom and Tony rode across it, would blow them sky-high.

Tom had okayed the action but when the director read it he demanded Tom use doubles for himself and Tony. Tom refused. The director asked, "Is Tony insured?"

Tom triggered back. "Your kids insured?"

"It's a little different, Tom."

"Not to me. How could money replace Tony? Besides, insuring him might be a jinx."

Tom mounted Tony, waved to the dynamiter who was going to do the detonating and galloped along the narrow trail.

As they neared the blow-up point a dust particle blew into the detonator's eye. Quickly flicking it out, his vision blurred, he pushed down the plunger thinking Tom and Tony had passed over the dynamite. It blew up just as they rode over it!

Tony lay still as death beneath Tom, a bleeding wound in his side, his legs bent, not a tremor from him as the pain mounted, not a whimper or moan. Tony might have lurched up but he waited until his beloved Tom was taken from beneath him.

They brought a stretcher for Tom. He refused it, waiting for an attending veterinarian to administer a sedative and assure him Tony would live. Only after all possible aid had been given his little pony did Tom let them rush him to a hospital.

Most of the folks who worked with Tony considered him human. He certainly acted more like a human than a horse. He had the temperament of a big star and displayed it on the slightest provocation. One day Tony kicked up his heels and Tom, trying his best to get him into line, just walked off and left him.

Tom had just hired a three piece orchestra to "mood him up" for his thrillers and also to keep the crew and players in a happy frame of mind. As they struck up a popular tune Tony trotted over and stood listening. In a matter of minutes his tantrum was played out and the wonder horse was again making the day's shooting a bull's-eye.

I remember one day when we were working out in sandy San Fernando Valley someone forgot to bring the orchestra and Tony started acting up. From a nearby farm the prop man dug up a portable phonograph and soon Tony's ruffles were smoothed down. And forever after a phonograph went wherever Tom and Tony went.

Tony was a thoroughbred in heart only. Jet black with a white blaze on his forehead and white sox on his hind legs, he *was* Tom Mix in horse-flesh. They rode the highways and byways of the world. The streets of New York, Paris, London and Berlin echoed to the cheers of the crowds that had come to welcome them. The one time Tom didn't ride Tony, the most terrific cowboy in the world rode to his death in one of his high-powered cars, outside Florence, Arizona, in 1940.

Placing Duke, the Great Dane, as a footnote to the legend is not a slight. Tom loved the Dane as much as his horse. Many scenes in his epics featured Duke, and the goings-on between Duke and

Tony as they tried to steal scenes from each other were in the tradition of the movies' greatest thespians.

Tom decided to settle this drama-match once and for all. He wrote and directed a film titled *Teeth*. Here is the review of that struggle of the equine against the canine.

"Tom Mix's 'toot ensemble' has been augmented by Duke, a dog. With Tony, the cowboy star's horse, the animals carry the burden of this western melodrama, built around the hero unjustly accused of murder and his faithful hound getting the goods on the real culprit.

"Every situation features the dog. Still it seems as if he knew a little too much even for a dog. He can spot a hub cap on an automobile and lift keys from a jailer's pocket. Eventually he helps the hero to rescue the girl from a forest fire—a scene effectively thrilling. Not much hard ridin' here. Mix does away with his usual exploits to give the dog a chance. And Duke can make a big bark over his performance."

Tom had this to say about this film:

"There is great rivalry between Tony, my horse, and Duke, my dog. Each feels himself the star of *Teeth*. I, myself, according to their point of view, am only one of the cast.

"There's a good deal to be said on both sides, when it comes to their relative importance. Tony, of course, claims precedence because he has already starred in his own story—*Just Tony*. He feels that Duke is nothing but a beginner.

"Duke, however, has worked with me in seventeen pictures—which is quite as good a record as Tony's.

"The truth is that they are both wonderful workers. I know that a lot of people, watching their almost human actions in *Teeth*, will think it must be the result of a lot of training. But that isn't so.

"I never have trained Tony, nor have I taught Duke any tricks. I have owned both since they were youngsters. Painstakingly at times, I have showed each just what I wanted him to do and they both have understood. When it comes to training, as understood by men who do this kind of work, Duke and Tony know nothing. They are just smart, well-behaved horse and dog.

"One day Duke sprawled his massive body on the floor of a set at the William Fox West Coast Studios, with absolutely no expression in his eyes. There seemed to him to be no reason for an expression.

"Then he saw me as I walked in. There was the wildest excitement. Duke almost deafened the bystanders with his barks. I went over and patted him, and then sat down beside him and we had our morning 'sing.' It was highly satisfactory to us, but Director Blystone and others on the set happened to think of something they had to attend to elsewhere."

Tony and Duke made personal appearances with *Teeth* during its Eastern run. Tony got the jump on Duke by having a manicure and permanent wave of his mane for their performances at the Paramount Theatre in Brooklyn. Duke, a short hair, called it sissy stuff and settled for a bath and a brush-down. But Tony, some recalled, got just a little bigger hand from the audience as they took their bows from the stage.

Tom, Tony and Duke . . . their shadows stretched from silent to sound and now television runs. And why not? They were the biggest three in talent, heart and triumph.

19 TWO BURROS TO A BONANZA

In 1905 Clarence Jones was delivering groceries for his father by foot, in Edendale, California, where Mack Sennett later built his mirthful monarchy.

An overweight teenager always called "Fat," the young boy decided there must be an easier way to get food to his father's customers. Passing a Mexican vegetable wagon drawn by two burros one lazy afternoon, he found freedom for his sore feet—and he changed the course of his life.

Later his father sold the store and Fat traded his cart and burros for his first horse, Chick, a buckskin colt. Not long after he bought and broke another colt, Buck.

Watching a Pathé flicker company shooting a 1912 two-reeler in the Edendale hills, Fat approached the production manager, offering his horses for sale. He sold them on the spot with the stipulation he ride them in their films for twelve dollars a week. The bonanza showed its first vein.

Over fifty years have passed since the young boy stopped walking and started delivering. His million dollar ranch in San Fernando Valley has furnished films with thousands of four-legged breeds in hundreds of movies. Many of his horses have gone on to stardom. Rex, King of the wild horses, Flicka, Blanco, the white stallion of Green Grass of Wyoming; King of TV fame.

"I look at a thousand horses to buy ten, and only four or five will ever make it in pictures. I don't care how good a judge of horses you are, you can't tell, until you've tried him, whether he's going to take the training. Kinda like the humans, I'd say.

"I don't believe horses think things out. They remember from repeating the trick over and over and always being rewarded when they perfect it. I let my trainers use whips but only as cues. Sometimes we use a ten-cent store water-gun to squirt at them to remind them they aren't obeying."

As to favorites, Fat claimed he never had any but many of his wranglers remember his affection for Sunny Jim, the versatile mount that Texas Guinan, later Queen of the Night Clubs, rode in so many westerns in 1918.

"You can't help but like a horse that goes out and does anything you ask of him, but you don't dare get fond of them. This is strictly a business."

But as Fat recalled Sunny Jim his eyes wrinkled and he had a little trouble with a cigarette. Fat, old-fashioned, liked to roll his own.

"A gentle little bay, Sunny Jim could do just about everything. I felt he was headed for the big time. He was also sure of himself. He knew exactly what was asked of him and always got the action on one take.

"That last day he was doing something he'd done a hundred times—galloping along a moving train and letting his rider jump on the car. Give him his head and he'd put you alongside the train and stay with you until you were safely over." Fat had now finished the roll and lit the cigarette, his hand trembling slightly. "I'll never know what went wrong. The guy must have tried to check him in, when he should have let Sunny do it. His head was pulled against the train. The rider lived and Sunny died. It was such a waste of great talent . . ."

Rex, King of the Wild Horses, in a still from *Wild Horse Stampede*.

William Janney and Dorothy Appleby bring supper to Rex, the wonder horse.

Rex, King of the Wild Horses, was the first horse to be starred on his own without the help of a human big name. A vicious bay stallion, he had been mistreated as a colt and never forgot it.

Fat had him brought from Colorado by Jack Lindell, one of Hollywood's leading horse trainers. Lindell had to halter and hobble him. So the first horse star was chained to his orbit.

But this wildness and defiance of the world fascinated movie fans. A shot of Rex racing across the floor of a desert valley was worth the price of admission. So was a raging fight with a mountain lion. Black Beauty charged with lightning, Rex had no rival past or present.

"Rex made plenty of money for Hal Roach and he was quite a personality. But he never got to where you could trust him. Rex was a mean horse to the end. Like some human actors are mean."

A long ride for the fat boy who started with two burros and a cart. He had gained money, fame, and recognition as movieland's greatest discoverer of horse talent. What does it all mean?

"Not a thing. If I hadn't been lucky I'd still be trading anything on four legs. And I guess I got a soft spot under my hide for horses. No sentiment and mush. Strictly business, like I said. If it weren't, these critters would run off with all the profits."

Mr. Plutarch for a footnote to the saga of Fat Jones . . .

"Nothing made the horses so fat as the king's eye . . ."

20 AN IRISH HUNTER WENT WEST

Handsome Fred Thomson, a former minister of the Gospel, discharged from the army in World War One in 1918, visited with a friend who owned a riding academy in New York City.

A beautiful Thoroughbred Irish hunter, named Silver King, attracted Fred. His friend mused.

"You and Silver King in Hollywood would be a hit, only trouble is—this stallion's mean as the devil."

Fred smiled.

"I never was afraid of the Devil. Let me take him for a ride in the park tomorrow."

Everything went well until they rode into the park. Silver King tried to tear Fred out of the saddle by ducking under a low tree branch. He bucked. He whirled. But he couldn't throw his rider.

Using an old cowboy trick, Fred *threw* Silver King. Tieing his legs with the end of a rope he administered a sound spanking to the proud white stallion. The rope's end didn't hurt him but Silver King yelled bloody murder. People crowded around and someone called a cop.

Let up on his feet again, the Irish hunter hung his head in shame. He clearly realized he had met his master and a friend. And as Fred patted his nose and gave him a sugar lump love shone in his eyes. In the heart of this touching scene the law arrived and demanded to know what was going on; but when Fred explained, all was serene again in the park.

A week later Fred Thomson and the Irish hunter went West.

The magnificent white stallion was a sensation. Most of the equine stars were Western mustangs. Silver King stood in a class by himself. The Irish hunter and the movie camera clicked beyond all of Fred's hopes. In rehearsal the horse wandered listlessly through the action, seemingly bored stiff. But the moment when the director shouted "Action;" "Camera!" and he heard the click of the boxed-eye, he was on fire with performance. Sometimes he ad-libbed excellent business. Fred was never able to explain it, how the click of the camera turned Silver King into a John Barrymore.

Fred Thomson and Silver King.

Like the Great Profile he was temperamental and only Fred could bring him out of a tantrum. Silver King hated doubles. The first time a double was used he attacked the horse and disrupted the day's shooting. It was incredible how he knew when another horse was doubling for him. Another time, despite the fact Fred had taken Silver King some distance from the set, he broke his halter and plunged over a cliff into the water below, just after the double had done the stunt for him. There was only one solution— when a double was used Silver King had a day off.

Silver King waits for a rider in this scene from *Jesse James*.

Silver King was good copy for the gossip columnists and the slightest display of his temperament was headlined. And the morning Fred rode him onto the set with the Irish hunter wearing specially fitted dark glasses, the newshawks swooped down en masse. What kind of horse wears sun glasses? Can a horse really be that human? What was Fred Thomson pulling on the public? Was his horse making a fool of him?

A few days later Fred Thomson released the following story:

"Silver King, after working on some night scenes, began to show signs of blindness. I took him to a veterinarian and after a thorough examination, he stated the horse had the "scourge of the studios"— Kleig Eyes. The bright lights were causing temporary blindness. The usual treatment of cold cabbage leaves was given him and we kept him in a darkened stall for ten days. He has entirely recovered but must wear dark glasses when acting before the Kleigs."

"Fame is the spur that the clear spirit doth raise . . ."

21 THE BRUSHBEATERS

The movie industry's demand for animal actors had people pulling their laying hens off their nests, butting goats from their milking, parrots from their perches. When their pet cages and backyards were empty they took to beating the brush in the Hollywood hills.

Mr. and Mrs. Orval Rounds sent their two girls through college by renting out their trained skunk. The skunk wandered out of the brush near their hilltop home one dawn and Mr. Rounds, having a way with animals, invited the smeller into his fold. Deodorized, Emmy, the girls called her, after an amazingly brief schooling, was on continual call.

A prop hand at Universal Studios in San Fernando Valley, Wally Ivers, trained his son's white mouse to run up an actor's leg. The mouse, as a comedy gag, created a sensation and Wally retired from manual labor to manage his movie mite.

Mary Jane, a goose who came to Christmas dinner but captivated the hearts of the Luckett family, stayed as a guest and almost forced dentist T. J. Luckett to abandon his life's work.

The goose, displaying extraordinary talent, under guidance from the children learned to talk, sing, count up to ten and walk around in an old pair of the doctor's shoes. When the children saw Bozo, "the goose of a thousand gags," in a Sennett two-reeler they demanded their father offer Mary Jane to the nearest picture company. Mary Jane, proclaimed the Luckett kiddies, could act feathers off Bozo.

Like a good father Dr. Luckett obeyed his children and to his surprise Mary Jane was hired the first time out. When her salary reached $20.00 a day—a four hour day no less—the Lucketts had a conference: to drill, or to manage Mary Jane? As the doctor looked over the many accounts unpaid he decided to split his duties: he would work three days a week as Mary Jane's manager and the other three as a filler of cavities and pain-killer. Dr. T. J. Luckett was the most versatile oral surgeon on the movieland scene.

Nadine Dennis, a legal secretary, had been given a beautiful parakeet called Parita. She performed a variety of tricks that amused and amazed Nadine's friends. When someone brought a casting director to the house for a party, he immediately latched onto Parita and begged Nadine to let her work in a current Gloria Swanson society-drama. Nadine let the bird appear more for a joke but Parita's talents were highly appreciated and she was always in demand as a subtle and decorative touch to many a cinema triangle or a cute comedy relief in heavy drama.

But the price of fame sometimes comes high. Catching a cold on a drafty set, Parita went to bird-heaven in short time. Nadine loved the little feather-merchant so much she had her stuffed and she was a conversation piece for many years at many a social gathering.

In the early Twenties a conservative estimate by the various studio property departments placed at least 200 people in and around Hollywood enjoying a comfortable living supplying films with a variety of animals.

But what happened when exotic locales in pictures required unusual and rare animals? Not many folks had an octopus for a pet or a thousand grasshoppers in their backyard. And how can you be friendly with a vulture?

Two young Englishmen with imagination, Archie and Stafford Beckingsale, offered the answer. They opened the Famous Pet Exchange and boasted they could fill any movie need from any part of the world.

Their business card read: "ANYTHING FROM A BEE TO AN ELEPHANT."

For Cecil B. De Mille's 1927 classic, *The King of Kings,* they provided 1200 white pigeons. Not a spot of black was to be seen anywhere, thanks to C.B.'s drive for authenticity. A hundred doves had to be found, and a dozen buzzards. And then there was the vulture that clawed the cross of the unrepentant thief on Calvary.

A Ruth Roland serial called for six hundred grasshoppers and they supplied them at the flat rate of two dollars a dozen for the *Queen of Danger.*

A Raymond Griffith comedy, *Wedding March,* almost stumped them when a pigeon as a climax of the plot, was to steal a priceless pearl necklace.

Over 300 birds tried out and failed to pick up the pearls. Archie and Stafford huddled in a dark corner of the stage. Their future depended on their boast. Had they met a Waterloo? What do pigeons like most? Frankly, they didn't know or know anyone who did. Their diet was fairly conservative. Could they have found one odd ball, say, in number 301?

Real champagne was used in the scene, this was the custom when directors sought realism. Archie's eyes glinted at the bottles in their iced buckets. Maybe—Stafford shrugged his shoulders—may as well try anything.

Dipping the pearls in the giggle water they reached for number 301. Everyone was on their toes watching as the camera clicked and the pigeon pecked at the pearls, batted his eyes, and then, as if plugged into a wall socket, grabbed up the gems and flew out the window.

The competition among animal trainers to find talent became as acute as that among the trainers of human actors. The ballyhoo and rainbow-promises manufactured by both were equally persuasive in luring the movie aspirant into their cages.

Jack Allman was the ambitious owner of an animal casting office. His problem: no animals. He had opened with a few strays and half a dozen pros but he lacked star material. So he started advertising, becoming the first talent scout to explore this field of discovery. His copy ran like this:

"Hollywood's Noah's Ark. We'll make a star out of anything that walks or crawls on legs or anything else. No experience necessary. No fee for training. Usual agent fees.

"Some of our urgent needs for immediate work in glamourous Hollywood:

> One fifteen foot snake, breed open, for gag business
> One pig, stout who can wear light make-up for night work
> A swarm of bees—not camera conscious
> One goat who can learn to butt backwards
> One cat who can learn to swim any style

"Don't feel sorry for the animals you see on the screen. Hollywood is kinder to dumb creatures than to humans. Animal performers are carried to and from the studios in automobiles and are especially fed while they are working. Never any overtime. Those death scenes are carefully faked. Trained animals are too valuable to be exposed to danger or bad treatment. Mortality rate among human actors 100 percent above the animal. Cruelty is strictly against the rules, as it breaks the spirit of the animal and frightens him out of doing his best work. Small wonder two-legged players envy the four-legged.

"Who knows you may have a duck worth a fortune or a pet mouse that can be a star. Call for an interview and bring anything that's alive and doesn't talk. Absolutely no actors wearing *animal costumes* wanted. We sell only the real rats."

The stampede on, Jack had to hire extra help to sort out the star-talent from the starry-eyed.

One of his rare discoveries was a coyote—tame as a dog. He'd howl on command, steal dummy chickens, be the best villain the script called for.

Another was a police dog, who, aided with a little make-up, impersonated a wolf. His acting was so realistic that other police dogs shunned him when he came on the set.

Jack's favorite was a parrot, Gumdrop by name. Few understood this rather odd name for a bird. But when Gumdrop displayed temperament or didn't take to a human player and sometimes went for an ear, a gumdrop sweetened his bad temper and he acted his beak off.

Jack was one of the first to introduce deodorized skunks, but he had a hard time selling them to films. No one ever believed the smell had gone. And oftentimes a band of characters fled at the sight of the fuzzy wood pussy.

Jack had a tender spot in his heart for his buzzards and owls. Rarely were they called, and then only for something grim or shocking. And when a wise guy started stuffing owls and buzzards and renting them at half price, Jack's feathered group sank into slow decline. They'd sit on their perches from morn to night waiting for that magic call that came so rarely. When it did it poised a problem for Jack as to which bird to choose. Generally he simply flipped a coin to reach a decision.

In the Spring the following advertisement appeared in local papers:

Trained snakes, iguanas, Chinese dragons, grave robbers, horned toads, lizards, frogs, tarantulas, centipedes, bats and turtles—all broke and trained for picture work. What you can't get elsewhere, give me a call. Jack Allman, Court Auto Park, 219 N. Broadway, opposite Court House. Phone Main 2175.

"Reptile Jack," as movie folk later dubbed him, at the end of his first month in business showed these entries in his books:

Fox Studio: 2 crawfish, 1 baby snake, 1 lizard, 2 frogs, 1 horned toad......$15.00
Fox studio: 2 bullfrogs......$5.00
Fox studio: Rental 3 white rats and death of same......$6.00
Fairbanks studio: 1 king snake for 1 week......$15.00
Madison productions: 1 trap door spider for 1 day......$15.00
Jack White Co: Three days work locating 3 bull frogs......$45.00
Lasky studio: 3 rattlesnakes for 1 day......$25.00
First National: rental of boa constrictor 1 day......$100.00
Fine Arts studio: 7 bullfrogs man and car for 1 day......$15.00

Cecil B. DeMille had been Jack's first customer, the great megaphoner wanted two lively rattlers for *The Virginian*, starring Dustin Farnum. A dozen or so from other exchanges had failed to strike when C. B. wiggled his finger at them. As Jack let the rattlers out DeMille stepped forward. He waved his finger once and the snakes struck like lightning. Forever after Jack was in the DeMille fold. No

Cecil B. DeMille helps excite rattler for *The Virginian*.

one figured out why Jack's rattlers were always so lively since snakes sleep a lot and sometimes just won't perform. If they showed this tendency Jack sprayed 'em with a little whiskey just before he let them go before the cameras. It failed only one time.

Hurry up calls from the studios many times sent Jack on the hunt. His favorite hunting grounds were along the banks of the Los Angeles River. On hands and knees he would creep slowly along the banks of the "River of Many Jokes"; it rarely had water and only a heavy rainy season filled it, sometimes causing it to overflow its banks. Jack would scrape little bumps of sand with an open knife; in this instance he might be digging for tarantulas. After an hour or so the extremely agitated spiders would be trapped, in several bottles labeled and ready for their assignment—perhaps to scare the wits out of lovely Mary Miles Minter.

Jack's den of snakes, rodents and spiders was just around the corner from the Los Angeles County Court House. Here the deadly Gila Monsters, scorpions and chuckawallas snoozed in cool cages while unsuspecting Angelenos strolled by. There was never a complaint from anyone, and only the cramped space eventually forced Jack to vacate.

Claiming he could fill an order for anything that crawled, Jack was put to the test when First National, producing *The Lost World*, a story of prehistoric animals in South America, telephoned for a wood tick. They wanted a close-up of the bug frolicking on hero Lloyd Hughes's neck, but not one that would take up permanent residence. It seemed all other pet exchanges could not supply such an insect. What a challenge for Jack! As an afterthought, the property department said, "Get two, if you can, one might die!"

He hadn't owned or even seen a tick since he opened his doors. But he did house rabbits from the Mojave Desert. He picked those rabbits like a frantic monkey. No ticks. He visited his old standby— the Los Angeles River. Here he turned monkey again searching every bush and bramble, and even a herd of goats grazing nearby. It was quite a sight to a passerby—Jack going over those hides like he'd lost a gold piece in their fur.

The grapevine said no ticks anywhere in Southern California. This only spurred Jack. He knocked on private barns asking owners if he could search their livestock for ticks. One old fellow ran him off with a shot gun. But an elderly lady, when he explained why he wanted the ticks, became most cooperative and led her cow, Becky, out of the barn and into the blazing sun. She even helped Jack look. He found two in Becky's tail. In addition to a cash payment,

It's doubtful if this is really the rattler's last moment, because Harold Lloyd is toting the gun.

Jack promised the elderly lady he would arranged for her to visit one of the film factories.

With his ticks in a match-box Jack stalked into First National, and one of the fattest checks he ever received was for doing what comes natural to the ring-tails.

Fox Studio needed some buzzing insects for a little two-reel comedy—insects that would "make life miserable" for the comedian in a scene. "Get everything!" they told Jack. So, with a little box made of net, he headed out again for his old hunting grounds. He hit the jackpot: Wasps, yellow-jackets, grasshoppers, bees, gnats, butterflies, horse flies, house flies, katydids, mosquitoes, and some crawlers and fliers he had never seen before. Jack didn't see the picture when it was released, but if the comic ever let that flock of stingers light on him and go to work, he either laid off the rest of the year or jumped his contract.

Jack's longest search involved a bat Sam Goldwyn wanted for a movie. He hadn't even seen a bat since his boyhood in Iowa. He imagined himself climbing into two or three hundred attics or belfries. Sam wanted the flying fur-bearer in three days. Jack jumped on the telephone. He tramped the streets and stumbled through abandoned buildings. He tried a few caves a friend said he'd discovered in the Hollywood hills.

For the first time, almost at the breaking point, Jack picked up a conversation with an old timer who did odd jobs around an old ladies' home in East Los Angeles. Sure, there were plenty of bats in the attic. The old ladies would welcome him carting them off. It seemed the bats from time to time held nocturnal orgies in the upper areas and had the old ladies in a panic through the night.

Obtaining permission from the head of the home Jack climbed up on the roof around ten o'clock at night. As a bat winged out for some air he swung at it with a long pole with a net on the end of it. Once he almost fell off the roof. His first two nights he netted one lonely battered bat and knowing the studio he knew one of anything was never enough.

Jack called the studio and wondered if a day or so more could be obtained. The extension was granted since one of the stars was ill. Jack went back to his attic. After three hair-raising rendezvous with the crepuscular flying mammals, Jack had bagged five. When he brought them to the studio—you guessed it—they wanted five. The cost to Sam Goldwyn—one hundred and fifty dollars.

Jack had many humorous, almost tragic and sometimes embarrassing experiences but the one he most repeated concerned a hobo and a cootie.

For the 1925 World War I epic, *The Big Parade*, starring John Gilbert and Renee Adoree, director King Vidor added some humorous scenes of doughboys in the trenches trying to rid themselves of biting cooties.

Another hurry up call and Jack was heading for the Los Angeles River. No luck. He foraged under logs and then went barn-storming again. No luck. Was this to be his first failure? As the time grew near for the cootie scenes Jack in despair hiked down to the railroad yards.

In one of the jungles where hoboes congregated he spied a loner brewing some coffee in a tin can. With as much tact as possible, Jack asked the bum if he knew where he could find any cooties. The bum smiled, "How much you pay?"

Jack sputtered, "Five dollars!"

The bum straightened up and quickly removed his worn overcoat. "Mister, here's a start for you. And if you need any more I have a whole batch in my BVD's for another five."

Sometimes lady luck walked hand in hand with "Reptile Jack." Visiting the Lasky studio he wandered onto a James Cruze set, where a crisis had arisen. Director Cruze had ordered some cockroaches for a slum scene; the roaches were to scatter when a packing box was lifted. The property department had goofed.

But spying Jack, director Cruze hailed him over and offered him fifteen dollars for fifteen roaches to be delivered in fifteen minutes. At first Jack thought Jimmy Cruze was joking but when he realized production had come to a standstill he nodded and took off.

Walking onto another stage he paused on an old kitchen set, spotting some boxes and boards where grease had dripped down from the stove. Too easy. He'd been gone five minutes. Gently he rocked the boxes. Dozens of roaches scampered around his feet. But Cruze wanted fifteen and that's all he'd get.

"Jack, I'm changing your name from 'Reptile' to 'Magician.'" Or did you plan this with the property department to get more dough?"

As he laughed his way to the cashier's office everyone agreed Jack Allman was the top offbeat animal-man in filmland.

In his own words Jack summed up his unusual contributions to motion pictures and a summary of the actors who helped him carry out his fantastic assignments:

"There is no such thing as a trained snake, tarantula or Gila monster. It's only my experience in handling them and knowing what they will do under certain circumstances that make them appear as though trained.

"In *Wanderer of the Wasteland*, a rattlesnake is seen coiled at the edge of a water hole where Jack Holt, as a starving wanderer, lies face down to drink. As he spies the snake, he draws back and the snake starts gliding away, only to stop a moment later, wrap itself into a coil and viciously strike at him, barely missing his shoulder.

"I took that snake to the water's edge, its fangs had been removed, and placed it before the camera. Holt did his acting but the snake didn't. It just lay there. For more than two hours we waited for it to turn and crawl away, but it didn't budge. Finally I built a little brush pile in the rear, made a hole in it, pushed the snake partly in and pulled it out, pushed it in and pulled it out time and again. Then it began trying to get away from me. It wanted to get under the brush and stay there.

"I took it back to the water's edge and turned it loose. It had made up its mind its only means of escape was in that brush and so, when released, it beat it for the hole."

Jack Allman began handling snakes as a small boy on his father's farm near Eldon, Iowa. Often, his father punished him for bringing snakes to the house so he built a den and started collecting them. His first batch of forty he sold to a carnival company at a county fair for thirty dollars.

"That was more money than I'd ever seen before," he recalled. "So I continued studying reptiles and insects until I migrated to Hollywood."

"One of my best years supplying films I earned around six thousand dollars. And because I liked the actors I hired out I enjoyed my work.

"I go out into the desert every now and then for supplies—rattlesnakes, lizards, chuckawallas and the like. But for the tarantulas, yellow-jackets, smaller snakes, and insects, I couldn't get along without my little old Los Angeles River. And speaking of that river that everybody jokes about, one year it flooded its banks and washed me and a lot of other folks out of business. It can be a raging torrent when mother nature wants it to be."

William Campbell, one of the pioneer animal directors, was a close friend of "Reptile Jack." He recalled that no one had so many gags about animals for films or creating headlines.

While Campbell was directing at Sennett's, Jack brought him two Texas bull frogs. He told him they'd be a riot in a scene on roller skates. Campbell didn't believe it. A ballroom scene was being shot on an adjoining stage by Del Lord. Campbell spoke to him about the frogs and Del thought it would be a scream to have the frogs skate across the dance floor.

To add to the spontaneity of the gag, Lord didn't tell his players what was going to happen. As the dancers waltzed and whirled Jack rolled the frogs onto the floor and smack down the middle they skated. The dancers danced on. No one paid the slightest attention. Not a laugh. Not even a giggle. That's how the funniest gags in the world die, Campbell opined.

For a spoof on westerns starring the English comic Raymond

Hitchcock, Campbell remembered that Sennett wanted something funny with snakes in it. (Campbell didn't believe snakes were funny. The only time they got a laugh was in a Charlie Chaplin comedy, when as a drunk he attends a vaudeville show and watching a snake charmer act, thinks he's having the DT's, while in reality the snakes have left the stage and *are* crawling over him.)

Ford Sterling as the villain sells a suitcase full of snakes to tenderfoot-hero Hitchcock. "Hitchy," as he was called by fellow players, doesn't know what he has bought. As he opens the case in his room his girl knocks on the door and he has to stuff the squirmers inside his pants and shirt. His girl comments he has gained weight. Suddenly a snake's head pops out from his collar, another from his sleeve, another from over his belt. The heroine naturally faints. Mack Sennett seemed to think it was funny and asked for Jack to dream up another sequence.

Jack came up with a wild one. Hitchy goes to bed, winds up his alarm clock and falls asleep. Suddenly a rattler crawls up on the table and starts rattling. Hitchy sleepily reaches out to turn off what he thinks is the alarm, the horny tip of the snake's tail. It was original to say the least and Sennett thought it one of the maddest. So taken with the big rattler Sennett had Jack leave him around for a few days; maybe they'd dream up another hilarious bit.

Two weeks passed and Jack heard nothing from the laugh-makers. Generally when he left his charges for a few days someone would call him to pick them up or return them. For once in his life Jack Allman was scared, which was rare for a man who had been bitten a dozen or so times by the deadly ones.

He tried to reach King Mack by telephone. The King was on the set. Jack raced his old flivver fast as it would go and almost broke down the studio gate as the guard tried to slow him down.

On the set, the big rattler was coiled around the milk bag of a cow and Hitchy was about to milk the snake instead of the cow. Jack rushed into the scene like a wildman, grabbing the snake and stuffing him into a basket like he was a stick of dynamite.

Sennett stormed up.

"Sorry, Mr. Sennett. It was an emergency."

Sennett backed Jack up against the table.

"Well, Mr. Sennett, let me explain. As you know, I de-fang all my rattlers. But you've had Joe here so long his fangs have grown back. Another day and I'm afraid you'd had a tragedy on your hands instead of a comedy."

The End—of snakes at the Sennett zoo.

The brushbeaters have long since departed and their exotic breed with them. The modern movie seldom features a tarantula, gila monster or a swarm of wasps. Maybe the pesticides have invaded even the land of make-believe. . . .

22 THE FIRST LION OF THE SCREEN

When your performance eclipsed a star of the magnitude of Harold Lloyd, and you stole a scene from Mae West by taking her head in your mouth and you brought home $1,000 a week to your owner, W. J. Richards, you must be the first lion of the screen.

His career spanned the silent and sound eras in which he appeared in more than 250 pictures. He never had a name until his tenth feature, the 1922 scorcher *Burning Sands*, co-starring Milton Sills and Jacqueline Logan.

It was love at first sight between Jackie and the lion. And when she took to walking him around the Paramount lot, scaring the daylights out of everybody, Melvine Koontz, his trainer and life-long friend, decided his charge must be christened.

As he and Miss Logan went over a long list of names she suddenly got an inspiration. "Why not call him Jackie? I'd be delighted to have the king of beasts named after me." And so he was. Since he was a male it was odd but it seemed Jackie started a trend that has continued through the years, climaxing with the fantastic success of—Lassie.

"Jackie is the most human lion I ever saw," actors, directors and fans all agreed. He rode to the studio with Koontz in taxicabs. He ate in the studio commissary beside such celebs as Cecil B. DeMille who used him in most of his spectaculars. He frolicked at the beach with stars like Buster ("Tarzan") Crabbe.

Who said he was a lion? Stubby, his mother for one. And for a witness there was his grandmother Mamie. Both had starred for Colonel Selig in his early wild animal thrillers; Mamie was the first of her breed to act in a movie (*The Lion's Bride*). There was no mistaking that Jackie was a lion and with actor's blood in his veins.

But responsibility for the way in which he became the Clark Gable of the light maned Nubians rested squarely on Melvine Koontz's shoulders. Koontz had been employed as a jack-of-all-trades at the California Zoological Gardens in Los Angeles, where Jackie was born.

Gloria Swanson and Jackie in *Male and Female*.

"When he was about four months old, a studio wanted a lion cub to play in a picture and they chose Jackie. It was time for him to be weaned from his mother so that it was all right to take him from her. He was given to me to care for because he was used to me.

"I took him from Stubby, his mother, one morning and put him in a little red cage on wheels. I went at noon to see how he was and the sight of me excited him so that he banged his head against the bars. He carried the scars from their bruises to the end of his days.

"He gradually became used to his own cage but he was never in it for very long. I figured I would have to be with him as much as possible until he got over missing his mother, so I let him run loose and he followed me every place I went. He was even with me at night for a while. I had put a bed for myself in one corner of a shed and a box of straw in another corner for him.

"The first night we slept in our makeshift bedroom, I had no sooner dropped off to sleep when I wakened with a start. There was Jackie on my bed. From then on, for a month, he slept in the same bed with me and would curl up as close to my body as he could get.

"He used to be with me when I went to the lunch stand we had at that time, and this is an example of how smart he is. He saw me open the refrigerator door to get milk and in some way he learned how to open that door. He would stick in a paw and pull out a bottle of milk onto the floor. Whenever we found broken bottles and spilled milk we knew who had been there."

As with dozens of human actors Jackie won his claws in a Mack Sennett slapsticker featuring Ford Sterling.

Ford Sterling comes home slightly tipsy. As he opens the front door he stumbles over a cat. Swaying into the kitchen he sees Jackie lapping a bowl of milk. Slightly confused he finds a bigger lion in the living room. Going into the bathroom he bumps into a still bigger cat. Staggering frantically into the bedroom his eyes bug as Duke, the biggest lion of them all, is sleeping in his bed.

As Jackie turned two the owners of the Gardens realized they had a prize in the young lion when visitors continually swarmed around Koontz and the cub as they wrestled on the lawn for the fun of it.

The wrestling lion! It had never been done before. It couldn't miss. And it *was* a sensation in the Gardens' arena and led to Jackie's movie debut.

The act began with the lion and the man boxing. Jackie was the only growler any trainer would allow to slap him with an open paw. Koontz would be knocked down and he'd get up and start boxing again. Jackie would slap him down again and again, as the crowd roared.

His trainer commented that this unusually dangerous act was possible only because Jackie enjoyed it. It was fun for him. He had played this game since his cubhood and the thought of hurting his master never entered his head.

Following this they played "wheelbarrow." The trainer would pick up the lion's hind legs and steer him across the arena floor.

Next Jackie would "play dead." Koontz would attempt to rouse him, teasing him with a small whip. Finally throwing the whip across the arena he would instruct Jackie to fetch it. Jackie would ignore the command. After several demands from Koontz he would lazily rise and retrieve the whip.

Koontz would then reward Jackie by taking him for a ride in a wagon. Climbing in the cart himself, Koontz would instruct Jackie to push him around the arena. Slowly Jackie would rise on his hind legs; he would place his front feet on the back of the cart and then shove his master across the floor. The act ended with Koontz on Jackie's back riding him to the arena door like a pony.

What was Koontz's secret?

"People who watch our act get the impression we are just playing and that is perfectly true. I didn't train Jackie to do any of these stunts. When he was only a few weeks old I began taking him out every day for a romp on the lawn. I didn't teach him to wrestle, that just developed in our play. Jackie has grown up in that spirit of play.

"He will work with anyone. He likes his fellow workers. He is quite fond of greasepaint and likes to lick it off actors' faces. Perfumes delight him but music usually puts him to sleep. He lives on about fifteen pounds of meat a day and his favorite is vanilla ice cream in a cone.

"As to the more exacting stunts I double for the actor like riding on his back or jumping on his back from a tree or a building.

Jackie and Trainer Koontz.

"In *King of the Jungle*, with Buster Crabbe, a scene had Buster taking a bullet out of Jackie's back. I was offside calling to him, telling him what to do. When he walked into camera range I told him to 'play dead.' After Buster supposedly removed the bullet, I called him from the other side of the set and he walked out of the scene.

"I've trained many lions in my time but none of them were like Jackie. Jackie was terrific. No other lion like him in the world."

Like most people, Jackie had his human predicament. He was a loner; he had to be. His trainer felt association with other lions might bring out the beast in him and spoil his gentle nature.

Jackie never mated. But as his trainer stated, "when lions are mated they generally go bad."

So you can truthfully say that Jackie gave all for his art, and a film immortality few humans can equal.

23 THE M.G.M. LION

Breaking with Jesse Lasky and Adolph Zukor in 1916, Samuel Goldwyn formed his own company and one of his first official acts as head of the new corporation was to instruct a young advertising fellow named Howard Dietz to dream up a trademark.

Famous for his aphorisms even in those days, Sam quipped:

"I want something big enough and loud enough looking to be heard from the silent screen. And something that will scare off anyone trying to steal our product."

Dietz, still fresh out of Columbia University, reviewed the current trademark trend. Animals were leading in most film symbols. Only Edison used a human, Mary Fuller, one of his stars. Pathé had a rooster that crowed. Metro had a parrot that tossed the letters of the company name all over the screen. And the Bison was now bulling his way to fame for Colonel Selig.

Remembering the popularity of the Columbia University lion, Dietz predicted:

"What was good enough for Columbia should be good enough for Goldwyn."

Showing him the layout, the former glove-maker said:

"I like that cat. Call him Leo and make him a little more artistic around the mane."

Dietz, recalling a motto his Latin Professor always rammed down their throats, scrawled across the bottom of the sketch—"*Ars Gratia Artis.*"

Sam stared at it and then to Dietz's surprise, the unpredictable producer translated:

"Art is Beholden to the Artists."

As Goldwyn films rang up profits and popularity at the box offices across the land, Sam decided his company merited a "live" trademark.

Who posed for it? Several lions have been employed through the years. With the rather dubious name of Slats, the first lion to appear was a member of Gay's Lion Farm in Los Angeles. The forming of Metro-Goldwyn-Mayer brought Jackie into the trademark picture.

The world's most famous lion.

With the advent of Technicolor Tanner made the first splash in living color. For eighteen years Tanner had shared the lion roster with Jackie. In the twilight of the latter's career he doubled for Jackie.

Melvine Koontz, who also trained Tanner, enjoyed relating an amusing story about the good-natured cat whom he nicknamed "Mister Dependable."

"I can't use Jackie in a scene where people are running, because he playfully chases them. He thinks anyone who runs is inviting him to play. Tanner won't do that. If he is to go from one side of the set to the other, he starts out and never gives a look at anything until he reaches the place he is headed for. No matter how many persons are running he will not be distracted. He has a one-track mind.

"Something very funny happened while they were filming *Central Park*. In one place in the story the lion is supposed to run wild in a nightclub. He upsets tables and chairs and people run to get out of his way. I knew I couldn't use Jackie in this scene, so I prepared Tanner to play the role.

"I placed Tanner's cage on the opposite side of the set from

Nils Asther finds diversion frolicking with Leo Jr., son of the famous trademark beast.

where he was going to enter so that he could run across, straight into the cage.

"He entered the scene at the proper time, scrambled over the tables and chairs and ran from the set. But he was so intent upon getting into his cage that he mistook the camera cage for his, and rushed in. It was barely large enough for the camera man, his assistant and the camera, so that when Tanner bolted in, all they

Leo poses for the statue which now adorns the front of the **M-G-M Build-ing. The sculptor is Bert Levy.**

could possibly do was sit on him until he broke through some loose boards and reached his own quarters. We couldn't tell who was the more surprised, the men or the lion."

Time has changed many things at the massive M.G.M. citadel but the trademark lion remains as a symbol almost as famed through-out the world as America's eagle.

24 LOVE SCENE WITH A LEOPARD

For his 1919 drama, *Male and Female*, starring Gloria Swanson and Thomas Meighan, Cecil B. DeMille wrote in a scene with a leopard to tense up the jungle-island sequence. It was one that leading man Meighan never forgot.

"The scene shows Gloria hunting for food. Suddenly a leopard begins stalking her. About to spring on the unsuspecting girl I appear and with bow and arrow knock the leopard to the ground and then mercifully finish it off with a homemade hunting knife. Shouldering the corpse I head for camp with Gloria all aglow over me as her he-man rescuer.

"First C. B. tried a stuffed leopard for the finish. After one take he shouted: 'It's ridiculous, legs sticking out like posts, tail like its got arthritis, eyes like ten cent store jewelry, body as supple as a sack of sand. No, I've got to use the *real* leopard.'

"Her name was Minnie. She had been hired from a circus wintering in Southern California. Taking one look at us she had showed her fangs and was ready to spring at anything that moved on the set.

"C. B. assured Gloria and me cutbacks would be used and we'd not actually have to play the scene with her physically. All but one scene. As he turned to me I felt like Moses must have felt on Sinai. 'Tom, you'll have to carry her on your shoulders. No other way to do it.'

"An assistant reminded Mr. DeMille the studio had promised to return Minnie in perfect health.

"'Don't be a fool, man! I'm not going to kill her.'

"I said, shyly, 'Is there another way?'

"'Certainly. We'll chloroform her. And she'll be limp as a rag. I'm sure Tom this shot will go down in history. You and Gloria playing a love scene with a leopard wrapped around your neck.'

"We all waited nervously as a trainer slipped meat in Minnie's box and then as she ripped into it dropped several sponges soaked in the sleeping stuff through a trapdoor on top. She raged and ranted and clawed at first smell and then, after a brief struggle, passed out.

"I slowly shouldered Minnie, who started to drool on my neck.

Gloria took her place beside me. C. B. called for action and camera. It was a long scene, I think the longest scene I ever played. But C. B. loved it and kept encouraging me and adding dialogue as we walked through the jungle. Suddenly I heard a rumble in Minnie's belly. I felt her breathing on my neck. An assistant on the sidelines shouted Minnie was coming to. C. B. shouted him down and said keep up the action. Her mouth opened. Her teeth scraped my shoulder. I hesitated a moment. C. B. yelled to go on and not worry about Minnie. Minnie's claws began to unsheathe. I almost dropped her. But another roar from C. B. and I staggered on through the tropical vegetation. How I ever registered any love for Gloria I'll never know. The climax was reached when one of Minnie's claws drew blood on my thigh. I heard C. B. clap with joy and then, oh, then, thank the dear Lord, he yelled: CUT!

C. B. was all over me like a kid at a circus. As I looked at the trainer carrying Minnie to her box I wondered if picture-making was really worth it. I also wondered what C. B. would try next.

25 JOE MARTIN

As one of Universal Pictures' biggest stars in the 20's, ranking with Priscilla Dean, Frank Mayo, Lon Chaney and Mary Philbin, Joe Martin was naturally envied by his fellow-players. When a thoughtless executive mumbled during a production conference: "Talent? We got only one actor on this lot with talent—Joe Martin." The storm broke.

Actors don't mind being told other actors are prettier or handsomer than they are. Even comparisons in popularity don't raise the blood pressure. But when an actor is told he hasn't as much talent as another actor—and if that actor is an orangoutan—atoms separate!

Now, what about Joe Martin? Did hatred and gossip and discrimination affect his performances? Did his health suffer? Did he have to lie on a couch? Nothing happened to Joe except success and more demands from Curly Stecker, his manager and trainer, for more privileges.

Joe had the first portable dressing room. Joe had the first closed set. Not even Carl Laemmle, head of the studio, could watch Joe act unless he asked permission of Curly Stecker. Joe also had his meals on the set, refusing to eat in the commissary.

Naturally this had a tremendous impact on the other stars. One actress screamed she'd break her contract if she didn't get a mobile dressing room. A prominent male star when told his next vehicle was opposite jolting Joe headed for Palm Springs. A week later he returned to play a second lead to the redoubtable ape.

One critic wrote:

"Joe Martin would seem to stand forth as the greatest and most convincing argument the Darwinian theory has ever known. It does not tax the imagination to think of Man having evolved from the like of Joe."

Joe carried on, turning out smash portrayals, outdoing himself in roles that few of his tribe ever matched.

Joe's only human weakness was temperament. If his lunch arrived a few minutes late Joe might express his rage by almost dislocating the caterer's arm. Of course Joe didn't know his own strength.

His charm and ease with female players broke the boycott. The ladies found him more a gentleman than the gentlemen. Of course when they cajoled him by trying to outdo each other for roles in his films, Joe's head swelled. It was as if he were saying to himself, "you are really special now."

His manager broke the bad news. Joe would not work after four in the afternoon and there was to be absolutely no night work. And there would be no publicity spreads. So Universal went ape, because it had a box-office bonanza.

Male players always acted under tension with him. He relished this, flexing his muscles, performing fantastic athletic tricks just to make them look pitiful by comparison. He challenged anyone to put the gloves on for exercise—no takers. Joe smiled and swaggered back to his portable dressing room for brunch.

Joe wasn't an aristocrat though his ancestors tailed back to the doorstep of Eden, but whenever he did such a role, he revealed unusual understanding of the finest in manners for both drawing room and table. His dipping of a soup spoon brought mouth-watering praise from all over the country. Attacking a juicy sirloin, he had

Jim (Tarzan) Pierce and Dorothy (Jane) Dunbar pose with Joe Martin.

Joe Martin brings "Lightning Lizzie" in for a pit stop.

the poise of a brain surgeon. His handling of a Havana would make any onlooker take a deep breath, inhaling and relaxing as Joe did.

What was Joe's secret? He loved being a movie star. He loved the sound and the fury. He loved himself as much as his fans loved him. Joe was born out of context. He should have been two-legged without arms that made it appear he had four.

Most bedroom and bathtub splashings were performed by the females. Joe was a male exception. Every picture showed him in bed or in a tub. Audiences would burst into applause as he winked at them and pulled the covers over his head or lathering heavily dunked himself in a sea of suds.

His endorsement of a Murphy bed upped sales 25 per cent.

But as always with classical and sometimes tragic heroes, a bathtub sequence sealed Joe's doom.

A three year old baby boy wanders into the bathroom and tumbles into the water-filled tub which his mother has prepared and then is called away by the ringing of the telephone. Joe, passing the bathroom, hears the baby's cries and leaps in saving the baby.

A simple scene for the great Joe Martin.

But Joe had been suffering from the sniffles and having to do the scene many times due to the baby's inexperience, his cold worsened. In twenty-four hours Joe was suffering from pneumonia and as everyone at Universal, including Uncle Carl Laemmle, waited, Joe fought for his life.

Joe won his battle against the grim reaper but he was never the same. He forgot his lines. His moods deepened. He even turned on a couple of his female leading ladies.

A conference of all the studio heads was called.

Cal York in his column, "Gossip—East and West," wrote a final tribute to one of cinelandia's greatest short-hairs.

"Joe Martin, beloved of the theatre-going public and adored of screen patrons, has run amuck. In other words, he has gone bad. And so Universal has sold him, for $25,000 to the Al G. Barnes Circus—where he will be a headline—behind bars.

"Joe Martin, as everybody knows, is a monkey. He has served the screen long and faithfully. We can't hate him for going crazy. It was over a year ago that he was put in solitary confinement, and labeled unsafe. We can't help feeling that there are a good many people that might join him—and yet the world doesn't place them in circuses.

"Where's justice, anyway?

"Goodbye, Joe. You were not handsome, but you were one of our favorite actors . . ."

26 ME CHEETAH, YOU TARZAN*

The thrill of the Tarzan movies has always held special attraction for me since I worked with the first Tarzan—Elmo Lincoln. As D. W. Griffith dubbed him after he'd rounded up some real wolves that had escaped from the set of *The Last Drop of Water*, shot in San Fernando Valley, "Elmo, you're a living Tarzan."

In researching and questioning directors and trainers and actors about the many Cheetahs who helped enliven and humor the Ape-Man's exploits, I have discovered that monkeys are very difficult to interview. It seems they have never taken the press—or anybody else—seriously.

But what chronicle about the celluloid animals would be complete without the Cheetah stories?

So here they are, after much research and attempted personal contact, as I believe they would tell of their experiences.

For obvious reasons real names are not used. The public has always thought of them as "Cheetahs" no matter who played the part.

"Since I was the first Cheetah I certainly feel I have the right to speak first. After all I have both age and a good memory to qualify me though my experience was the saddest of my flicker career.

"After Elmo Lincoln scored such a big hit in *Tarzan of the Apes*, in 1918, the jungle hero's star started swinging across the Hollywood landscape. A second film, *Romance of Tarzan*, with Enid Markey again as Jane, hit the jackpot.

"The character of Cheetah didn't appear in either of these silents. Guess they felt a Chimp might do a little scene-stealing. And Jane was the top female interest, and as all of us know, the human female is jealous as a green-eyed lizard of a Chimp female. I know that sounds catty but what can you expect from a monkey.

* Permission to reprint the quotations in this chapter granted by Gus Spathias, publisher of *Mosaic Magazine*.

"In late 1919 Goldwyn pictures began casting for *The Return of Tarzan*, and the call went out for Chimps by the treeload for the newly created role of Cheetah. Harry Revier, the director, put the gals through all kinds of tests but as I watched his face I was convinced he hadn't found the right swinger. And I knew why: the chimps were all acting like ladies, at least trying to. Cheetah was female but hardly in the lady class. When my turn came I just acted crazy and ended up by stealing Revier's megaphone out of his hand and clamping it on my head like a dunce cap. Guess who got the part?

"Was I all a-chatter that first day of work! The peak of my career—playing opposite the hottest male star in flickers—Elmo Lincoln. What a chest that man had! Darken his hide a shade or two and grow a little more hair on certain spots and Elmo could have passed for the best looking gorilla in the jungle.

"When my manager and I arrived on the set—no Elmo. Well, a big star had a right to be late. Maybe I'd be late, someday. Nervously I started re-doing my nails. All of a sudden I saw a leopard skin walking and I jumped shrieking into my manager's arms. A second look—it wasn't a leopard but a shuffling man wearing a leopard hide. First off—I loathe leopard skins whether on floors or leaping

Elmo Lincoln in *Adventures of Tarzan* with Joe Martin.

through trees. My manager pinched me in a tender spot and I slid out of his arms and waited as director Revier led the leopard man by the hand over to us.

" 'This is Gene Pollar—our new Tarzan. He used to fight fires for the New York City fire department.'

"No Elmo. I sighed disappointedly. Well, that's movies, I thought.

"I looked the new Tarzan over and shook hands. Seemed to me like it would take a fire to get him up a tree. As for a chest—oh, my.

"I don't mean to be mean about Gene Pollar. He was a perfect gentleman. Maybe that was what was wrong. He tried hard—too hard. He fell out of a tree like a rock. He got tangled and almost strangled in ropes supposed to be vines for him to swing on. I think he missed his ladders a little.

"Revier almost turned the picture over to me—close-up after close-up. There were scenes in which I had even the crew laughing. And then the last laugh. Revier had me sitting on a log going after a bunch of bananas. He had me balance one on my nose and then catch it in my mouth as it fell. He had me toss one in the air and catch it in my mouth. He had me peel and eat one and almost gulp it down in the same breath. Finally he shot enough banana-business and everyone was aching from belly-laughs including Mr. Pollar. Revier came up to me and said I was a second Charlie Chaplin and hearing that I felt I had come of age as an actress. My heart leaped in my mouth and I jumped four feet in the air and landed smack on the pile of discarded banana skins behind the log. I also dislocated my disc and my career in the same fall.

"I never played Cheetah again. And my remaining years have been spent in and out of small circuses, even a zoo that folded from lack of customers, with always this barker-talk or a sign on my cage— 'Tarzan's first Cheetah—she liked bananas not wisely but too well'. . ."

As the first Cheetah's collaborator I feel I should footnote her sad reminiscence.

The Return of Tarzan was lambasted by the critics and Gene Pollar was ridiculed. Edgar Rice Burroughs himself called the picture a stinker. A jinx had followed it from the start. A year or so later it was booked into theatres under the new title, *Revenge of Tarzan,* which hardly changed the caliber of the film.

But the first Cheetah had come into her own.

The futile search for a suitable Cheetah to play in the fifteen-chapter serial, *Son of Tarzan,* also directed by Harry Revier, ended with a midget dressed up like a chimp acting the part.

Soon after the serial opened its weekly runs throughout the country protests poured in denouncing the hoax. A petition signed

Cheetah relaxes in director's chair.

Swimming champ Buster Crabbe was a later-day Tarzan.

by all members of the International Order of Chimps to Create Better Understanding with the White Ape was submitted in person by its recording secretary. The amazing young chimp so impressed the producer and director they hired her on the spot to play Cheetah in Elmo Lincoln's final appearance in another fifteen-chapter serial, *Adventures of Tarzan.*

Here is how she recalled her screen debut.

"The last thing I wanted to be was an actress. Oh, I'd been in one or two school plays and in a church pageant, but an actress, it never entered my head. But as the recording secretary of the IOCCBUWWA, it was my duty to stop this masquerade of a human midget as a chimp.

"I never could have done it without Elmo. Elmo—dear Elmo—he was so kind and chivalrous. I was terrified in front of that cranked-up box. He told me it was just a machine and harmless without the cameraman's hand.

"Many times during the action I stepped out of camera range and Elmo would always gently yank me back into place. If I forgot my business he always led me aside and rehearsed it in private. Once the director swore at me, saying I was acting like a human and not a monkey. I thought Elmo would tan his hide. Without Elmo I never could have done it.

"Of course, that Louise Lorraine, who played Jane, tried to cut my scenes to pieces and write herself in even when my back was to the camera. But director Bob Hill finally stood up for me and handed me more chances to get giggles and laughs.

"Miss Lorraine never once laughed at me. She was always objecting to something in my scenes with her and Elmo, saying my love-sick looks in their love scenes were completely out of character. How could a chimp love a man! I was tempted to have a copy of the many such relationships we have in the classified files of the IOCCBUWWA sent to her on the q-t, but when I discussed it with the heads of our organization they felt it might embarrass a few people still living and their families.

"*The Adventures of Tarzan* was a big success; I was offered a long-term contract but motherhood stopped that. Even afterward they wanted me. But without Elmo I just couldn't play Cheetah. Too bad I had only a family of sons. Still, what about this dog, Lassie, being played by a male?"

When sound sidelined many a reigning star in Hollywood it only enhanced the appeal of the Cheetahs. Their delightful squeals, screams and special dialogue—highlighted by Tarzan's blood-curdling yell—made the film jungle seem real.

And a final interview with one of the last of the star-Cheetahs.

"I know I am probably the most disliked Chimp in Hollywood. But can I help it if I starred with two of the top Tarzans—Johnny Weismuller and Buster Crabbe? And can I help it if critics have written me up as the greatest Cheetah of them all? And can I help it if I got the part because I was the only chimp in the world to match stroke for stroke Johnny and Buster in our own crocodile-infested pool? And can I help it that when Sol Lesser producing one Tarzan

Johnny Weissmuller: perhaps the most famous Tarzan of them all.

epic and M.G.M. the other, had to use me in *both* pictures? This is the first time I have revealed this sworn-to secret. But what other actress, human or otherwise, ever did that?

"It seems headlines always followed me no matter what I did or didn't do, which of course, is typical of all great and glamorous stars.

"Well, during the filming of the 1932 *Tarzan, the Ape Man,* directed by wonderful Woody Van Dyke, who made the immortal *Trader Horn* in Africa, we were on location at Toluca Lake, north of Hollywood in San Fernando Valley. Years later Bing Crosby built a mansion there.

"I hadn't been feeling up to par and it was a windy day and by the time the crew had everything set up, I began sneezing. It was a scene where I ran up to Maureen O'Sullivan, who played Jane, and kissed her after Tarzan had saved her from some awful dwarfs.

"I held the sneezes through several rehearsals. Miss O'Sullivan kept forgetting her lines. Right in the middle of the first take I sneezed in her face just before kissing her.

"Miss O'Sullivan looked at Woody. Woody looked at me. I sneezed again. Miss O'Sullivan fled the set. My manager quickly walked over. I always had a stand-in. We hardly used her. Maybe for long shots or a fairly dangerous stunt. I sneezed again. My manager motioned for the stand-in.

"While they wrapped me in blankets and hustled me off to a car taking me to the hospital, I watched the stand-in giving herself the last once-over in a mirror. A close-up. At last she was getting a close-up. What she didn't know was that the close-up would be of the back of her head. I giggled through another sneeze as the car drove off.

"Three days later I returned to work. I looked around for the stand-in. Everyone was dumb when I asked where she was. Finally I pestered my manager to tell me what the big secret was all about.

"It seems in the rush of the scene and the excitement, a strand of Miss O'Sullivan's hair got in the stand-in's eyes, blinding her temporarily. The stand-in went berserk and bit her!

"I almost broke my sides open laughing. As I say I am the most disliked chimp in Hollywood. And the highest paid one, too. And not in bananas—hard, cold cash.

"A most unpleasant experience also happened during the shooting of this Tarzan epic. Since the talkie rage was on, everybody talked—including the Sphinx, Garbo. I wanted to talk too. I dropped a few hints. The script girl said even Johnny didn't have any lines yet. One day I heard to the contrary. In a scene with Jane, Johnny grunted and said: 'Me Tarzan, you Jane.'

"I blew up. I demanded that Woody let me have a scene with Johnny saying, 'Me Cheetah, you Tarzan.'

"The producer was visiting the set. He really lashed out at me. Woody tried to cool the fire. I spit at the producer and walked off.

"I was the best, don't you forget. But that was my last film. They found another chimp. Oh, they cut her part down. And Cheetah became more or less a low-comedy relief. But what do I care, I can live it pretty darn high on those TV residuals!"

The star-system for Cheetahs took a back seat. Chimps were used less and less and in *Tarzan Goes to India* not at all. It seems a pity. Because there are no greater performers in the entertainment world than monkeys and their relatives. And how can you blame the simian for mimicking the ways and manners and temperament of his fellow players when it has been written:

"So men were developed from monkeys of course"—Lord Charles Neaves.

27 WAS DARWIN RIGHT?

The rarest of all animal pictures were produced by William Fox, Educational and Tiffany pictures. A few independents also contributed to the flurry for the furries.

These films had all-animal casts. Dogs, monkeys, fowl. Their before-the-camera histrionics amazed everyone. They were almost as incredible as the time and patience the humans gave to capturing these performances on celluloid. For a span of years, silent and sound, these delightful comedies caught on at the box-office and vied even with features for popularity.

Here are a few reviews reprinted by permission of *Photoplay* magazine.

Darwin Was Right produced by William Fox. 5 reels, 1924. "Fox comedy monks do it again. In their latest comedy they take up the current American craze—the game of Mah Jongg. The scene where Papa, Mama and Baby try to master the intricacies of Mah Jongg is one of the funniest in the film. Maybe our human actors could get some fresh gags hiring the writers who dream up these side-splitting monkeyshines.

"Here is a flight of fancy that for the first time uses human actors with the famous monks. The plot involves two scientists who invent a Serum of Youth and by its use are enabled to meet themselves in former incarnations. But it is the monkeys who do not feel flattered by the theory of evolution and steal every scene from their human co-stars. Akka, who stole a whole feature film from Syd Chaplin titled—*The Missing Link,* also steals this one even from his tailed brothers. His performance is marvelous, making you almost forget he hails from treetops."

Chasing Around, produced by Tiffany. 2 reels, 1931. "Maybe you're one of those anti-evolution critters and don't see anything funny about chimpanzees that look and act ridiculously human. And, on the other hand, maybe you aren't. In which case you'll get a kick out of the latest effort of Tiffany's furred comedians.

"It starts out with a family quarrel, in which the son—with an English accent that will panic you—attempts to act as peacemaker.

Then father and son go for an airplane ride that is among the funniest ever filmed. The lines crackle wisely, and the acting of the chimps is something to see. Have a look at this if it comes your way."

A Fowl Affair, produced by Educational. 2 reels, 1931. "Here is a real novelty—something you have never seen before. Moreover, here is a real comedy, with all the actors either ducks, chickens or geese. They move about a miniature town, drive miniature cars, wear miniature human clothes and have full-grown human voices.

"The plot concerns the greatest love of Elmer McIntosh, a poor country boy, for the great stage idol, Genevieve Longhorn, and the villainous designs of Red Miller, a 'bad egg.' In other words, a burlesque of hokum melodrama. The way the fowls—much harder to train than any animals, strut their stuff will not amuse you, but amaze you. The making of this film was literally a case of not rubbing the feathers the wrong way. It required all the tact and ingenuity of the trainers to smooth down the temperamental goose and chicken stars in the Fowl Comedies Co."

The most revered and honored of all animal films was produced by comedian Ken Murray, *Bill and Coo.* It won a special Academy Award in 1947.

28 TO BEE OR NOT TO BEE

J. Searly Dawley began his career which eventually led to being a writer-director-producer of some of the silent movies top hits at the Edison Film Company in 1906.

With *The Phantom Honeymoon,* Dawley gave the silver screen its first shot of "special effects." The story: a young married couple on their honeymoon around the world.

Dawley used background shots taken from the four corners of the globe and then played his characters up against them. It was startling and proved the young man was as inventive as his boss, Thomas A. Edison.

A stickler for realism he went to incredible lengths to create mood, setting and in one case—a swarm of flies. The scene took place in a country store for Marguerite Clarke's starrer—*The Goose Girl.*

The storekeeper goes to a sugar barrel to scoop out some of the sweet stuff for lovely Marguerite. As he lifts the lid a cloud of flies pops out and a funny scene follows.

But it was December in New York and flies do not reside in the nation's largest city in December. But an alert animal trainer got 100 bees from a farm in a neighboring state. Who would know the difference? Dawley went along with it.

Placed in the barrel the bees refused to budge. The trainer put an electric fan in the bottom of the barrel. That would rouse them. When Dawley called for camera and action and the fan was turned on the bees swept out, and in buzzing rage attacked everybody on the set.

But quick action by the trainer held the injury list to a minimum. He simply opened a window and the cold, wintry air rushed in; the bees fell to the floor, numb.

As Dawley surveyed the tumbled scene he smiled. It was all very funny and his cameraman had caught it in one take. And in that melee, the bees looked like flies.

The trainer gathered his bees and put them in a box, and as soon as the window was closed and the temperature rose they were as frisky as ever.

Dawley mused thoughtfully—To bee or not to bee.

29 STRONGHEART

In 1460 John Fortescue wrote: "Comparisons are odious."

Since the birth of movies from the casting director to the producer the question regarding new talent has always been: "Is she another Dietrich? Is he a Gable? Who does she look like?"

No one has taken the slightest notice of Mr. Fortescue's cogent words, which have proven their worth so many times when comparing presidents, artists or film stars.

Applying his advice to two of the most famous animal actors in all cinemaland—Strongheart and Rin Tin Tin—you can readily understand the wisdom of his statement. They had one thing in common: they were German Police dogs. But their individual talent was as different as day from night.

There have been many imitators: Rin Tin Tin Jr., Flash, Peter the Great, Kazan, Chinook, and others.

Because Strongheart was the first great dramatic canine to be starred in a feature film, he merited first billing.

As in many human careers, in 1921 one picture, *The Silent Call*, skyrocketed Strongheart into the film firmament. Never before had audiences seen a police-trained German Shepherd dog as the hero of a full length picture.

The story originally appeared in the *Saturday Evening Post* under the title "The Cross Pull" by Hal G. Evarts; it was a tale of a canine half wolf, a quarter coyote and a quarter dog who saves a girl, kills the man who attacks her, and brings her and her lover together.

One of the most compelling elements in the exciting film was Strongheart's love for a she-wolf. As they mate and have a family, the wildness in the dog appears to be satisfied. But tragedy stalks the little family. Strongheart, kissing his puppies goodbye, goes hunting for food. During his absence a nearby dynamite explosion seals off the cave in which his loved ones are waiting.

The scene when Strongheart returns with a duck in his mouth for their dinner and stands staring at the sealed cave and drops the duck in the rubble will live long in movie memory. Slowly the

Strongheart was an early canine champion. This drawing is by Rose O'Neill, who is also the creator of the Kewpie Doll.

shocked dog sinks to the torn earth and, staring at the tomb in which his family has been buried, tears stream from his eyes, his nose sinks into the dust, his entire body quakes with despair.

From the first to the last reel Strongheart dominated the action. The human actors were just there to lend support. The picture drew raves and long lines at the box offices across the country. Another Hollywood trend had begun.

With the man-and-wife team of writer Jane Murfin and director Larry Trimble, the dog from overseas became the dog of the world in such thrilling sagas as *Brawn of the North, The Love Master,* and Jack London's classic, *White Fang.*

In 1920 Jane and Larry decided to produce a series of dog dramas, and with the backing of First National Studios began a search that ended in Europe. After watching hundreds of animals parade before them, and almost despairing of finding a lead for their stories, they journeyed to Germany.

The canine line passed before them and again it looked like they had drawn a blank. But suddenly there was an animal that didn't march like a dog. Three years old, weighing about 115 pounds, he moved more like a soldier. Larry immediately saw him as the hero of his films and Jane agreed he was a magnificent specimen. When they talked to the trainers their hopes were dimmed.

Born in Germany, the son of Nores von ker Kriminal Politzel, an undefeated champion of his time, his kennel name was Etzel von Ceringen. Trained to kill with his fangs as a soldier with a bayonet, he could leap over any six foot adversary upon attacking him. He was as deadly a four-legged fighting machine as man had ever invented. Even his handlers never knew when he might turn on them. Like a grenade, he waited only for the signal that an enemy was lurking ahead.

The dog had never played with a boy. He had never known the fun of retrieving a ball or a stick. He had never been petted. He had never felt a man's arms around his neck. He had never nuzzled the soft sweetness of a woman's palm. He had never romped the fields or chased a bird or its shadow.

He had never been a dog . . .

Most animal authorities agree that animals—even the wild ones that man hunts down—want to be friends with man. Sometimes they accept even the explosion of his rifle as part of the jungle sounds that rally with the rhino's thundering hooves, the lion's roar and the elephant's trumpet.

As a lover of animals all his life Larry looked into the steely eyes of the military killer and felt he could take that muzzle off the dog's outlook on man and life. He saw the animal as a human being. And at the same instant, Etzel von Oeringen saw in a man's eyes something that didn't tighten his muscles, snarl his mouth and bare his fangs.

How Larry Trimble and the new-named Strongheart achieved this miraculous change was their secret and deservedly so.

He once said: "When you are with an animal, never be surprised when he does what you ask, even when you ask the first time. Always expect the impossible to happen. This will help you more than it does the animal. If there is no response, that is always a sign that *you* need more education yourself. Not the animal."

Strongheart's influence was tremendous throughout the world.

His fan mail proved him as popular as the ranked stars of the day. He enjoyed autographing his photos for fans. He achieved this by placing one of his front feet on a special ink pad and then pressing it down in the lower right corner of the picture. Strongheart relished his celebrity and the joy he gave to his human fans. In some way he sensed he was a pal to all the millions who didn't have a dog.

As the first canine to act as eyes for the blind in a motion picture, he inspired the forming of schools to train his breed in this highly specialized and noble work.

Like other luminaries, he met and fell in love with the beautiful Lady Jule. He sired many sons and daughters who later followed his star-dusted path across the screen.

But the dog who had begun life trained to kill, but who now had the world loving him and his kind, was shadowed by a grim fate that sometimes tracked down those who seek the film dream to end all dreams.

While acting out a fight scene he fell against a hot lamp and a blister formed. At first examination and treatment the burn seemed harmless. But weeks later a tumor formed and death's final fade-out followed.

In one of the most distinctive books ever written about and to an animal, *Letters to Strongheart*, J. Allen Boone revealed the fascinating facets of the dog star's intrinsic nature:

> I will share with you something I found out about him that revolutionized my thinking about a lot of things. Something that ought to be helpful for every human that appears in front of audiences. Let me begin by saying that one of the things in the Strongheart pictures that puzzled and baffled me was the acting of some of my friends. Ordinarily these actors were capable "troupers" either in stage or screen plays, but whenever they appeared with Strongheart there was a decided slump in their work. At first I thought it might be due to pride, that deep within themselves they were professionally ashamed of having to play subordinate roles to a dog in an "animal opera." But when they assured me that they liked acting with the dog, I knew I would have to dig deeper.
>
> One day I made what to me was an extraordinary discovery. Those actor friends were doing the best they could with the roles they were portraying, but their best was not good enough to keep up with the pace being set by the dog. Strongheart was not only outperforming them, he was making them look amateurish. He was running away with every scene he appeared in, and there was nothing they could do to prevent it. The moment the dog appeared, audiences lost interest in the humans. He rose above and dominated the story, the members of the cast, the production, and even the scenery.

Watching him from behind a continuous question mark, I gradually began discovering his "success formula"; and the more I found out about it, the more I began to understand why he had such universal appeal. What counted most in this "formula" was not his outward appearance, impressive as that was. Nor his unusual intelligence and the remarkable things he was able to do with it, although there were contributing facts. It was his character. His integrity. His attitude towards life. The fine things he stood for inwardly and outwardly.

I hunted through a dictionary and made a list of every good quality I had ever seen percolate through him in public and private life, noting particularly how he used them. It was a revelation. The list running into many, many hundreds; and remember, every one of them was a quality of the highest excellence. I did the same thing with my human actor friends. Then I compared the lists. The reason for the dog's superior drawing power on the stage and in motion pictures was as plain as day. He was making better use, more consistent use of his qualities in both public and private life. The humans had the advantage over him in such things as intellectual education, technical training, experience, the speech arts, and the use of make-up and costumes. But the dog was outshining them from the inside! And that inner radiation "packed 'em in," wherever he appeared, or his pictures were shown.

The humans and the dog were using different methods in their stage and screen work, and getting different results. The humans were in the habit of giving of themselves in varying degrees, depending to a great extent on the play, the part they were doing, their opinion of director and cast, and the state of their feelings and emotions. True, they were sincerely interested in the mental and physical efforts they were putting into their parts, but with it they were mixing an even greater interest, an interest having to do entirely with themselves; an interest concerned with what their particular part would do for them in the way of self-satisfaction, applause, reputation, money, press notices, fame and career. "Kingdoms divided against themselves," so to speak.

Strongheart, on the other hand, was perfectly coordinated within and without. He had no divided interests. No objective ambitions. No jealousies. No envy. No pettiness. No temperament. No ill will. No ego urges. No pretense. His main purpose was to get all of himself into outward circulation. To move constantly from the center of himself to his circumference. He was always looking for opportunities to share himself. When he found them he let go with everything he had. Like all dogs he never gave less than his best, never gave less than his all. I never knew him to cheat in matters of this kind. He always made full use of his capacities. He put on just as fine a show playing with an old shoe in a backyard with no one looking on, as he did when doing dramatic feats in front of wildly enthusiastic audiences. He was always as much of his complete selfhood as he knew how to be. And remember he was supposed to be "only a dog."

His inner goodness and its outer expression were so genuine and so appealing that men, women and children of every nation, starved for the things he was diffusing so generously, turned to him so naturally and as instinctively as flowers turn to the light.

They couldn't help it. He had what they wanted, what they needed. I doubt if anyone ever turned away from him unsatisfied or unnourished. People thought they were watching an unusually well-trained dog doing unusual things. What they were really doing, though, was looking through a moving transparency on four legs, and seeing a much better universe than the one they had been living in . . .

30

"THE WOLF SHALL DWELL
WITH THE LAMB . . ."

"The wolf shall dwell with the lamb, and the leopard shall lie down with the kid . . ."

Larry Trimble must have been meditating on these lines from the Holy Writ when he inserted the following advertisement in newspapers circulated throughout wolf country:

"Wanted: wolves to work in motion pictures. Top prices. No training necessary. Send animals or information to Larry Trimble, Denver, Colorado, U.S.A."

Studio officials learning of this wondered if Trimble had lost his mind. He explained he needed a pack of man-eating wolves for two Strongheart stories and was determined to get them.

And did he get them! Trappers, hunters, trading posts, zoos and ranchers all shipped the most ferocious cargo of graytails that ever rampaged the snows from Montana to Siberia.

Out of the snarling, battling mass Larry chose twenty-three of the most photogenic and shipped them to Canada, where a sprawling stockade had been built.

A few days after arrival, as Larry and his assistants watched the fights going on between the wolves to determine a leader, suddenly a sleek, silver-gray female, weighing about eighty-five pounds, began knocking off the other ladies right and left. Deep hacking fangs, wide-gaping jaws, slashed with a precision and beauty of movement that fascinated Larry.

"Lady Silver," he murmured. "That's what we'll call you—Lady Silver . . . and you'll be the only female wolf star in Hollywood."

As the males watched Lady Silver take charge of her sisters, they quickly fell into line after a few snarling passes from her. The Queen of the pack enthroned, Larry made his first dramatic move.

He moved in with the wolves!

When his shocked assistants insisted he at least take a rifle, he shook his head. "They'll think I've come to kill them instead of live with them."

Long a student of the graytails, Larry knew the wolf had been maligned more by fiction than fact. He really wasn't such a beast.

Lady Silver did much to improve Wolfdom's image.

Puzzled by man he wanted to get along better with him and, when offered human friendship, the four-legged animal proved as affectionate and obedient as a domestic dog.

The assistants shook their heads, the people of the nearby village tapped theirs. "It's dangerous business," they all mumbled. What if the wolves resented Larry and decided to kill him? Did he want them to shoot or pray?

Larry grinned, "I'll just have to take that chance. But if anything serious happens I don't want any of you trying to be heroes for my sake."

And so began the strangest experiment in pioneer movie animal history. Larry ate, studied, and slept in the stockade. The wolves dug holes at night in the snow and then crawled in for their slumber. Larry dug a hole too; he added only one human comfort—an Arctic bedroll.

On their own the assistants took turns at a night-watch that first tense twenty-four hours. All they heard were wolf and Trimble snores.

Larry began by throwing bits of his food to the wolves. They'd snatch it up and slink away. For days they just watched the man and he watched them. None of them showed resentment toward him. In those strange and ominous hours Larry put down their every movement, reaction, play, behavior with each other. He even noted the times and length of their sleep.

From time to time Lady Silver would venture from the pack, and standing off a few paces, study the man. What a magnificent creature she was! A true female and yet eighty-five pounds of ripping dynamite.

One morning as Larry prepared his breakfast Lady Silver sniffed to within a few feet. Larry held out a choice morsel. Slowly she crept toward him, each step loaded with a leap that could have slashed him to pieces. But the hand that held the food never trembled and finally, Lady Silver quite calmly nibbled it out of his fingers.

Outside the stockade the assistants and a few curious natives stood spellbound by the sight of a she-wolf eating from a man's hand.

The following day the Queen of the pack brought several friends with her. Three days later Larry and the wolves supped together. To make things quite cozy, that night the graytails dug their sleeping holes beside their man-friend, snoozed a paw's reach from him.

As time passed Lady Silver showed high intelligence and perception—and affection almost human for Larry. She seemed to sense that he would guide her into another world—a world not of snowy wastes that hunger and fear continually bloodstained, but a world of warmth, safety and the love a female felt when she bore her pups.

The morning dawned quite unexpectedly when Larry informed his assistants and the villagers he was taking his wolf pack for a romp—outside the stockade!

Strange as it seems no one showed any signs of fear or trepidation. They had seen what Larry had done *inside* the stockade, so why could he not do the same outside its confines?

Slowly the gate was opened and slowly, as Larry beckoned them, the pack followed him outside. First he played with Lady Silver; soon the others romped, ran and rough-and-tumbled. An hour passed and when Larry clapped his hands for their return, the pack tailed him into the stockade like lambs.

"The wolf shall dwell . . ."

As friendship grew Larry named the rest of the pack. Gay Girl . . . Inyo . . . Red Dog . . . Trixie . . . Mono . . . Flash . . . Lobos . . . Mike and Ike . . . Sibe and Tommy . . .

Eventually dogs and other humans were introduced to the carnivores and they learned to roam and play together. Now Larry Trimble was ready to storm Hollywood with his wolf-pack!

Never-to-be-forgotten scenes . . . The pack stalking down humans to kill them . . . Blood-curdling fights between dog-teams and the graytails . . . Strongheart, with Lady Silver at his side, standing off a fight to the death . . .

How Trimble accomplished these amazing sequences only he could tell. Hollywood and the fans were struck dumb. No human or animal ever suffered injury by the wolves. And the wolves seemed to enjoy their captivity. Their love of Larry Trimble was a thing to behold as he fed and petted them after they had done a terrific piece of acting.

Naturally Lady Silver was singled out. No female star ever conquered filmland like this Queen of the snows. And did she love it! The clicking cameras, like so many other animals before her, transfigured her, sparked something magical inside of her. She did things that even female dogs of long experience and training didn't do. She became world famous and changed a lot of opinions about the wolf in general. She was never temperamental. She had only one soft spot—she did not appreciate being whistled at.

"And so the wolf did dwell with the lamb—in Hollywood . . ."

31 THE MORTGAGE-LIFTER

On the morning of September 15, 1918, Corporal Lee Duncan, with a small party of enlisted men headed by Captain George Bryant, left Toul in Lorraine, France, to look for a new field site for the 136th Aero Squadron.

Near noon they stumbled on an abandoned German war dog station that had been heavily shelled. In a blasted dugout Duncan discovered a half-starved mother dog and five puppies. The Captain and the Corporal knew they couldn't stop the war for the cold- and shock-shivering little family and yet . . . The Corporal suggested taking them back to the hangar; the Captain nodded his approval. On the detail's return from the tour, after struggling with the mother who thought they were going to kill her babies, they rescued the litter.

That tattered second on the battle-torn wastes of No-Man's-Land was going to prove to be one of destiny for many people.

Many times asked why he suggested saving the little family, Lee said, "It was my mother, I am sure. Like I heard her voice even out there. When I was a kid she always reminded me to be kind to animals. She said, 'A boy who loves animals can love people twice as much.'"

At the war's end Duncan brought back two of the puppies while Captain Bryant took the mother and remaining three. Duncan named them Nannette and Rin Tin Tin after the finger-length dolls the French soldiers and airmen always carried with them for good luck.

Disembarking in New York, Duncan had to leave Nannette behind because she had contracted pneumonia. In Chicago he received a wire she had died. Considering her smarter than Rin Tin Tin he was deeply shaken by her passing. As the troop train continued on to California Rinty snuggled up to his master and licked his face. It was a million dollar kiss he never forgot.

Out of that mud-hole Lee Duncan had snatched a movie star that would one day earn more than a million dollars. Known as "the mortgage-lifter," because of his fantastic drawing power at

Rin Tin Tin shows off his equestrian talents.

the box-office, Rin Tin Tin was the property of Warner Brothers Studios in the lean days and, before and after sound, the star who held off the creditors. Insured for $100,000 he had his own production unit and several hundred men and women made a good living working for a dog.

In such Twenties' hits as *The Night Cry, Clash of Wolves, A Dog of the Regiment* and *The Man Hunter,* Rin Tin Tin ran the gamut of emotions as capably as any human star of the period.

And he lived like one as Joel Sayre commented:

"Rin had his own valet and chef, and his private limousine and chauffeur. The Warner's technical staff was as eager in his service. Every Rin Tin Tin epic was climaxed by his arrival to the rescue in the nick of time, so that he was frequently called upon to leap full speed through closed windows. To safeguard Duncan's priceless property from having his beauty marred or his jugular severed by glass fragments, windowpanes of translucent candy were contrived, and Rin sailed through them with breath-stopping effect. As a reward Duncan would sometimes let him eat fragments of the candy pane.

"Another wonderful stunt of Rin's was getting past a locked door by scrambling over its transom. Rin of course, could jump higher than any transom, but getting through one in a hurry was

Rin Tin Tin to the rescue in *Tracked by the Police*.

Rin Tin Tin comforts oldtimer in *Jaws of Steel*.

Rin Tin Tin is wide awake *While London Sleeps.*

Rin Tin Tin gets a stiff reception from a stranger.

always something of a tight fit for a ninety-pound dog. To make things easier for him, cleats painted to match the wood—thereby rendered invisible on the film—enabled Rin to run straight up doors with the speed of a cat. Using the cleats he could enter a second-story window or even go up a twenty-foot wall at top speed and get on a roof. When he had a scene involving running through fire, special chemicals were used to prevent his being burned. There were other technical marvels, too, to assist him in his breath-taking feats."

As with most movie stars the love-light shone in Rinty's eyes. The beautiful girl's name was Nannette and their marriage was a social highlight in the Beverly Hills home Lee bought for them and himself. As motherhood followed and Nannette presented Rinty with a batch of little ones a skilled nursemaid was hired.

Rinty had four sons who stood on their own feet as dog stars and Rinty IV became a sleeper-success on TV in a popular series.

Regarding Rin Tin Tin's amazing antics before the camera, Lee Duncan had this to say:

"Everyone has always wanted to know the secret of Rinty's training. He has never been trained. He's just an educated dog.

The screen's most famous German Shepherd looks around for action.

He may not have been human, but Rin Tin Tin knew how to celebrate July 4.

"A trained or broken dog wears a look of fear while he is performing his set tricks. He is afraid of the whip if he fails to do them correctly. Rin Tin Tin has never felt a whip. We simply understand each other and until you understand your dog you can never hope to teach him anything.

"The surest way of learning to understand your dog is to spend as much time as you can with him. Don't pet him every minute, but always reward him with a loving pet when he has done something well.

Sometimes other boys will tell you, 'Your dog is a coward. See him jump,' and they burst an inflated paper bag in the dog's face.

"Now that's no way to begin. There is no excuse for frightening him ever. If you want to teach him not to be afraid of the popping noise, try bursting the bag at a distance. Then come a little closer each time until he has gradually become accustomed to the sound and he will not be shocked.

"Dogs, like children, can't stand temptation, so when you go away and leave your dog in the house, don't leave your bedroom slippers on the floor for him to play with. If they are there, he will want to play with them and after a while he will play and chew too hard and when you come home there won't be any slippers.

Rin Tin Tin in classic outdoor pose.

"If you are careless enough to let this happen, don't scold your dog afterward, because he won't know what you are scolding him for. The time for scolding is when he is in the act of destroying the slippers. Then you may take him and say, 'Shame' or 'no,' and soon he will learn that the slippers are to be let alone.

"You will be able to teach your own dog many things as you begin to understand his ways and not until then.

"As to Rinty, I just understand him, sometimes I think he understands me more and that is why there isn't anything the director asks him to do he can't do. He knows he's a movie star and therefore must do his duty as such."

What was the extraordinary relationship between this man and his dog? Was it as simple as he has stated?

Rin Tin Tin cavorts with his trainer-owner Lee Duncan.

Rin Tin Tin gets a personally delivered Valentine from Audrey Ferris.

Rinty was a one-man dog. Only Lee Duncan could control him. After the scene had been taken he would be a different animal entirely. He might bite the very actor he had just played an affectionate and touching moment with.

Charles Hargan, who played fight scenes with Rinty, told Duncan one day that if the dog bit him he'd bite him back. Duncan laughed and then stunt man and dog did the scene. Following the rough and tumble Rinty suddenly bit Hargan on one of his padded legs. Much to everyone's surprise, including the canine celeb, Hargan grabbed Rinty and bit him on the ear. Duncan quickly rushed to the rescue of his walking gold mine. But Rinty learned a lesson. He never nipped Hargan again and Hargan continued as his adversary.

D. Ross Lederman, who directed some of Rin Tin Tin's outstanding films, described the fascinating union between Duncan and Rinty:

"With Lee handling him, there was nothing a human actor could do that we couldn't get out of the dog. Lee would tell him and we'd get it, often the very first time.

"He was always on time, never made temperamental difficulties and almost never blew a scene. There was a lot of black on his head and back, and we always had trouble lighting him properly in those

The faithful Rinty mourns a pal.

days. But I've seen him hold a pose for the electricians for thirty minutes without moving a whisker.

"It was amazing how he'd understand what Lee said to him. If there was a scene with four or five separate moves or actions in it, Lee would draw chalk marks on the floor—as we sometimes used to do for the human actors—and the dog would follow them perfectly. Lee never struck the dog nor lost his temper, and the dog had ears and eyes only for him. They always worked together entirely by love.

"Rin Tin Tin *was* Lee Duncan . . ."

As dramatically as Rin Tin Tin was born into this turbulent world he left it in his fourteenth year.

On August 10, 1932, after a playful twilight romp on their front lawn, Rinty jumped into Duncan's arms. He was dead weight. As Duncan fell to his knees he attracted the attention of his neighbor, Jean Harlow, who ran across the street.

As both cradled the beloved German Shepherd—born in war and ranging through depression and then reaching the summit of world popularity, acclaim and affection—his spirit passed like the shadows before the oncoming night. The screen's reigning love symbol Jean Harlow sobbed her heart out while Lee Duncan wept for a part of himself that also had died.

32 MARY OF M.G.M.

From the 30's to the 40's Metro-Goldwyn-Mayer was the biggest studio in the world and it boasted having "more stars than there are in heaven." It also boasted it had the biggest star of all—nine year old Mary, the rhinoceros.

Mary was imported from the great Hagenbeck Zoo in Hamburg, Germany, to star with Johnny Weissmuller in *Tarzan and his Mate*.

Mary was given the star treatment. She had her own bungalow on Lot Number Two with a fenced-in patio. Her food was specially prepared by an expert on rhino diet. Not even Marion Davies with her $100,000 chalet outshone this lady from Africa.

George Emerson, her trainer, who had worked with only two other rhinos previously, found the monstrous charge sensitive and good-natured. Every morning she would greet him in her patio. He'd pat her on the head and scratch behind her ears. Eventually she let him climb on her back and ride around the arena.

The studio dog, Teddy by name, came calling one day and Mary and he began a charming friendship.

Emerson finally talked to Johnny about getting acquainted with Mary. She took to him immediately and seemed to wait for his visits, which were infrequent because of the busy shooting schedule. But she never failed to recognize him.

The scenes in which Mary appeared had her meeting Cheetah on a jungle path and after Cheetah lets out a scream, Mary charges down on the helpless little monkey. Tarzan, hearing her screams, swings on a rope onto Mary's back and stabs her to death.

The director suggested a double for Johnny. Emerson warned that a total stranger would increase the danger. Mary knew Johnny and liked him. He didn't see any reason why she should mind him leaping on her back.

The director was still reluctant to take a chance on his valuable star. Johnny grinned and said, "Well, guess this is the time I have to prove I *am* Tarzan."

Lights! Camera! Action! Cheetah screaming! Mary charging!

Johnny Weissmuller's threatening pose doesn't phase Mary of M-G-M.

Johnny leaping! Trainer Emerson quickly roping Mary as she hit the side of a tree. And then gingerly as though it were a daily chore, Mary let her trainer lead her back to her bungalow.

Weissmuller recalled the spine-tingling scene: "It all happened so fast I didn't have time to get scared. Mary is quite a gal. I think she enjoyed the attention. I often visit her and bring her an apple. Sometimes I even ride her around the patio. She's Hollywood's most unique star."

33 IRAWATHA AND FRIEND

In 1935, Robert Flaherty, the distinguished director of such nature epics as *Nanook of the North* and *Man of Aran*, journeyed into the jungles of Mysore in south India to film, for Alexander Korda, a story based on Rudyard Kipling's classic, "Toomai of the Elephants," from his immortal *Jungle Book*.

As with all things Flaherty, the movie was an adventure featuring nature as much as the little boy and his love for the great elephant, Kala Nag. The camera laid bare the heart of India as only the master director could. Under the title *Elephant Boy*, the inspiring tale reached the screens of the world.

Four native boys were tried out to play the lead, Toomai. The final choice had a strange parallel. The boy's name was Sabu.

Sabu was an orphan, a ward of His Highness's elephant stables. When Sabu's father died, his elephant grieved; so they took him into the jungle where he disappeared. This true story was almost a carbon copy of the screen story. Who else but Sabu could play Toomai?

One of the most exciting and dangerous scenes had Toomai riding Kala Nag into a monsoon-swollen river. Several elephants were brought to the river for a tryout, where their mahouts commanded them to plunge in.

All backed away.

When Flaherty questioned the chief mahout as to whether the difficult swim could be made at all, he replied that there was a big tusker, Lakshmi Prassad, who might be able to do the job.

As the mahout mounted Lakshmi, Sabu scrambled up behind him. Flaherty told him to come down. The boy replied: "Sahib, if I am to be Toomai I must start right now."

For the first time in his directorial career, Flaherty wavered. Then he nodded his approval.

The elephant walked into the river and was swiftly pulled off his feet.

But he swam with head up and ears flapping. Suddenly the raging current caught him and tossed him up and under like a giant rag

Elephant Boy Sabu rides Irawatha.

Sabu wasn't so sure about Shere-Khan at first, but he now enters the cage without fear.

Irawatha gives Abut a boost.

doll. Sabu and the mahout fought the water rushing up to their
necks, Sabu once sinking out of sight. Tense moments were felt as
their heads bobbed above the current. The struggle of the beast
against the river continued. Finally, at a bend Lakshmi touched
bottom and as he stumbled onto the rocks the crew shouted and
burst into applause. Flaherty, cradling the dripping Sabu in his
arms murmured: "You are a star, my boy, in all ways."

Irawatha was the biggest pachyderm in Mysore, standing nine
feet, eight inches. He was the final choice to play Kala Nag.
But his heart and inborn intelligence eclipsed his size. It saved a
baby's life during a scene which called for Toomai and Kala Nag
to move through a crowded city street and the elephant to walk
over an abandoned baby.

As hundreds of sightseers watched the cameras rolled. Irawatha
lumbered toward the baby. His trunk down, he sniffed him. Slowly
he lifted his huge feet, which were thicker than the baby was long.
The first foot passed over the baby but the second foot struck his
ankles. The sightseers screamed and bedlam reigned. Rushed to the
hospital the baby was found unhurt. When Flaherty ran the rushes
that night he was amazed to see that as soon as the big tusker had
felt the baby's feet he shifted all his weight on the outer rim of his
foot, which saved the baby from being crushed to death.

Who says animals can't think?

During the production Irawatha went "musth" which sometimes
drives a male elephant mad. A white spot appears on the temple between the eye and ear and fluid oozes out. As Flaherty waited for
his magnificent pachyderm, fighting for his sanity, he decided to

Sabu trades jokes with Jiggs.

film the great animal's agonies.

Chained he struggled alone. He swayed back and forward. He swung from side to side. His eyes were blood-red with pain. He trumpeted to the heavens for help. For three weeks Irawatha was a mammoth of sweat and cry and then suddenly the madness disappeared and he became himself again.

Flaherty used these scenes when Kala Nag grieves for his dead master. They have never been matched by any animal in or out of captivity.

When *Elephant Boy* thundered across screens all over the globe, Sabu was voted a star and went on to incredible successes. And Irawatha? No record of the magnificent animal, who walking like a mountain yet having the touch of a feather in his feet, could save a baby's life.

Maybe like Clara Kimball Young's Lucky Dog, he returned to the jungle to live out the life nature had planned.

When Gene Towne and Graham Baker started casting the 1940 version of Louisa May Alcott's classic, *Little Men,* starring Kay Francis, Jack Oakie and Jimmy Lydon, the search for a bovine to play Buttercup, the most famous cow in literature, looked like it might rival the search for the actress to play Scarlett O'Hara in *Gone With the Wind.*

At breakfast one morning Gene Towne reached for a can of milk and discovered his long-sought star, Elsie, smiling from the Borden Milk label.

Starring for two years in the Borden Milk Company exhibit at the New York 1939 World's Fair, Elsie, born to the purple, wore her crown as the nation's bucolic belle with the air of a member of the exclusive Four Hundred.

She rivaled Elsa Maxwell as a hostess, with elaborate parties at the Roosevelt Hotel for three hundred newspaper and radio magazine guests, another for three thousand at the Bovine Ball. She autographed photos for the Finnish Relief with Hendrik Willem Van Loon as her escort. At the Hotel Astor, with the Governor and Mayor of New York State and City as distinguished guests, she thrilled the Inner Circle Political Writer's Show with a brilliant performance.

Born in 1932 at Elm Hill Farm, Brookfield, Massachusetts, of blue-blooded Isle of Jersey ancestry, Elsie was registered by the American Jersey Cattle Club as No. 998632 with the unusual name, used only among close friends, of "You'll Do Lobelia."

Her father, also having an unusual name, "You'll Do Volunteer," had contributed 266 progeny to the American bovine population and his 267th became his proudest chest-expander.

Her mother, called "Perennial Lobelia," held many awards and records for high milk production by the American Jersey Cattle Club.

Elsie combined marriage with a career in a most dexterous manner. Such famous cows as "Kingsway," Sea Lad's Milkmaid," "Jersey Volunteer" and "You'll Do's Best" rank on the top limbs of her family tree.

Everyone has seen the cartoon Elsie, but here's the real animal.

Weighing 975 pounds Elsie was one actress who didn't have to fear weight. Daily she ate forty pounds of food, which included seventeen items scientifically measured and mixed to provide nutritious milk.

Her first day on the *Little Men* set called for a scene in which Kay Francis was to milk Elsie. In a highlight of screen realism, the actors actually drank the milk massaged into the pail by Miss Francis.

Later the scenario demanded a dramatic climax for Elsie, in which she gives birth to a calf. When Towne and Baker mentioned this delicate business to Elsie's manager, he smiled back wryly. The

In this scene from *Little Men*, Kay Francis milks Elsie while Ann Gillis and Jimmy Lydon look on with interest.

producers hoped maybe another in their farm system could double for Elsie. The manager frowned. Elsie looked down her nose as she listened in on the conference. The manager retorted rather sharply.

"Elsie has no doubles for either acting, milking or motherhood."

Elsie and her manager exchanged coy glances as he continued.

"Only last week Elsie's personal obstetrician confirmed our suspicions—she will be a mother just about the time the picture is finished."

For once two Hollywood producers threw away their lucky rabbit's foot and patted the sides of the most cooperative cow in the world.

35

A LUMP OF SUGAR AND A PAT ON
THE NOSE . . . FROM ROY ROGERS

Hollywood, once cruel to its animal actors, has learned the far-reaching value of a lump of sugar and a pat on the nose. Of course, the lump and the pat come after the animal has done a good piece of work before the camera. But they reflect kindness, not brutality.

Kindness definitely pays off in animal training—particularly when training a horse. Intelligence and patience, too, play their parts in the training.

My pet palomino, Trigger, is a perfect example. Trigger, the most perfectly trained equine in films today, has not been subjected to cruelty. He has been handled with kindness, intelligence and patience. Glen Randall, who has helped me train my horse, understands what it takes to work with horses. Other animal trainers in Hollywood have a similar understanding, and that is why the old harsh methods of animal training have been abandoned in the film capital.

A horse must work on cue—learned only by hard work and patience. To my knowledge no clever horse was ever trained by cruel methods. Hollywood now recognizes this.

No acting animal today is subjected to harmful treatment. Nor are actors called upon now, as once they were, to jump from a second-story balcony onto the back of a galloping horse. Hollywood finally realized the dangers of such a stunt for the horse; it was comparable to the effect a man would experience from having a gunny sack of wheat hurled upon his back from the same balcony.

In *Roughly Speaking*, a squirrel was used effectively in one romantic scene. Do you think brutal treatment persuaded that squirrel, to do what what the directors wanted it to do? Indeed not. That squirrel, a valuable little fellow (for his earnings are high), is the property of Curly Twiford. And Twiford knows how to train such animals.

He also owns a couple of eagles that have worked in many pictures. And you don't get eagles to act by beating them or otherwise mistreating them.

I don't know much about squirrels and birds, but knowing some-

Roy Rogers and Trigger salute their many fans.

thing of Twiford and his work with his pets I am convinced they appreciate being treated well by everyone.

After Trigger and I complete a scene I always have a chat with him. And I think he knows what I say.

Gene Autry's horse, Champion, Tex Ritter's horse, Flash, and Bill Elliott's horse, Thunder, also probably know what Gene and Tex and Bill have said to them. These horses don't know cruelty.

In contrast to the earlier days of picture making, a humane of-

Roy, Trigger, and Easter. (That's the day he was born.)

ficer is required on every movie set when a horse is being used. Before the horse even sets foot on the set he is carefully inspected by a wrangler who is never permitted to have more than five horses in his charge. Then, if a horse becomes even the slightest bit ill a veterinarian is immediately summoned.

Horses, once led from studio to locations as far distant as 25 or 30 miles, now are transported by truck. Everything possible, as a matter of fact, is provided in way of good care for the animals.

For these various reforms, thanks must go to the humane associations operating in America—humane groups which protested the treatment once accorded animal actors.

These reforms have been good—just as good as that horse to whom I like to give a lump of sugar and a pat on the nose.

36 QUOTH THE RAVEN, "NEVERMORE . . ."

Curly Twiford never considered himself a literary man but that tell-tale line from Poe's famous Poem, "The Raven," read in High School, always haunted him. Whenever he lost a job—and during the Depression this happened often—he seemed to hear that old bird tapping on the door as it swung behind him . . . "Nevermore . . ."

Always a lover of birds and skunks and the more neglected members of the animal kingdom, he hobbied his frustrations away, training all sorts of creatures from gnats and guinea pigs to gila monsters.

Watching a Tarzan movie he suddenly asked himself a question: why not go into pictures? Not as an actor, but as a trainer of animals —animals nobody else could get and train. His slogan, which would tab him one of filmland's most noted gatherers of the skinned and horned actors, echoed his thoughts—"If it lives, I have it."

A pet Boston bull who did a balancing routine with two parakeets opened the movie studio gates for Curley. Soon he was known as the Jules Verne of animal-men. There wasn't anything he couldn't get. Or so it seemed.

"I thought M.G.M. had me once when they asked for twenty thousand ants for an African epic. But I started using my imagination and headed for Death Valley. Planting about five dozen mason jars by a group of ant hills I sat down and waited. In no time I must have had a million."

Anytime a live eagle streaks across a Cinemascope sky you can be almost certain it's Curley's fabled "Old Admiral." The largest captive eagle in films he had a spread of eight feet, four inches. An American golden eagle, Admiral worked like a canary for Curley. Many consider the eagle one of the impossibles. Curley did not. "Just patience and letting the Eagle know you're not afraid of him. That's all it was."

Despite his enormous success Curley still seemed to hear that old raven croaking on occasion. On one of his tours in the desert he walked up on a half-starved, half-dead baby raven. As he quickly gave the bird first aid he smiled to himself. *Now* he could end that haunter once and for all.

Jimmy and Coco receive promotions from each other.

When the 1938 stage hit, *You Can't Take it With You,* went into production an emergency call for a raven rang all animal trainers out of their beds.

The last call went to Curley, who had the only raven in sight or sound—Jimmie. Amazing Jimmie—a sleek shiny bird as photogenic as Robert Taylor.

Jimmie could do almost anything. He typed, operated a cash register, opened padlocks, lighted cigarets, selected an ace from a card deck with his beak, held it up proudly, slyly tucked it "up his sleeve" (beneath his wing) and then, waiting his chance, trumped your ace. Just call him Jimmie the card sharp.

In M.G.M.'s *The Green Years,* Jimmie outdid himself as the top raven in the movie cage.

His accuracy and speed were amazing. For any scene Curley would simply demonstrate the desired action; Jimmie imitated it. When director Brown questioned Jimmie's ability Curley accepted the challenge and he and the bird went to work on Brown. Jimmie arranged Brown's tie, tucked in his handkerchief, handed him a cigaret, took it back, picked out the proper coin from a handful.

In seven years Jimmie appeared in more than 200 films. He stood alone in a make-believe world where they had one Mary Pickford but tried to make a dozen.

Jimmie inspired Curley to do the impossible. When a new problem had to be faced Curley always repeated, with a minor change, "Quoth the Raven, 'Evermore'" . . .

37 CECIL B. DE MILLE'S TALKING TOADS

The greatest showman on earth, Cecil B. De Mille, was almost as famous for his film "firsts" as his spectacular productions. Imaginative and exciting usage of special effects, in both silent and sound, climaxed his epics. For example: the parting of the Red Sea in both versions of *The Ten Commandments* and John Wayne's fight with the giant squid in *Reap the Wild Wind*.

For a love scene between Paulette Goddard and Robert Preston in *North West Mounted Police* by the light of the moon on the Canadian prairies, De Mille conjured up the croaking of tree toads as a romantic pianissimo for the background. Quite a contrast to the leopard pulser in *Male and Female.*

Paramount Pictures "special effects" headman, Howard Joslin, did a little croak on his own when he received the order for the talking toads' sound track. What would C.B. think of next! His smile quickly changed to a grimace as he started his Hollywood safari in search of the *Bufo lentiginosus.*

He telephoned every pet shop on his list—no toads. Fish markets didn't seem to have phones, so he and his staff spread-eagled the smeller sellers from Hollywood to Santa Monica Pier, which noses into the Pacific Ocean—no toads. Aquariums! Surely aquariums would have some kind of toad. All he wanted was a chorus of croaks —no toads. Swamps! There must be swamps in Southern California, there was everything else. There *were* swamps. There were *no* toads. Someone suggested that perhaps toads haunt cemeteries. Equipped with butterfly nets and the reluctant permission of the headstone-head, Joslin and his crew prowled the Hollywood cemetery for several nights—no toads. But frantic calls from nearby residents, who swore Valentino was haunting the place, stopped further hunting.

One morning Joslin's office phone jingled a little louder than usual. C.B. calling. How was the toad sound coming? Joslin assured the master he'd have the toads in toe in no time. He just needed the right species for the correct Canadian accent.

As he hung up with C.B.'s laugh ringing in his ears, he wondered if these blasted toads were going to be his downfall. He recalled all the fantastic requests he had fulfilled, the challenges he had met and conquered. His ulcer became spiderish. He might lose his job. The phone seemed to barely ring this time.

It was the Hollywood Aquarium. From various cross-country sources they had learned that the toads could be ordered from a Florida hatchery—that is if he didn't mind something coming from Florida. Joslin shouted that he didn't care where they came from and how much the cost. Get them pronto!

During the week, while waiting for his precious cargo to arrive, Joslin read every book he could lay his hands on that covered the habits, manners and customs of the toad family. He actually felt a kinship with them. They weren't such bad little fellows. A trifle on the homely side but not as ugly as people thought. In a way their distorted features gave them a "character" so-called beauties never possess.

C.B. called on the sixth day. He even hinted he might sit in on the recording session. Joslin tried to discourage this by quoting experts who claimed toads didn't like crowds—only crowds of their own species. Shy creatures, they rarely croaked in numbers above a baker's dozen. C.B. chuckled and agreed to let Joslin go it alone.

The Hollywood Aquarium was calling again. The toads had arrived. Should they send them over? No, no, he'd pick them up. He'd be right over.

But Joslin's junket was delayed by another phone call for a hurry-up sound track for a Bob Hope-Bing Crosby "Roader." They wanted the sound of a cobra swaying.

Two hours later Joslin rushed up to the Aquarium—closed. He stared in the windows. Everything was locked up. Without realizing it he felt himself straining to hear the toads croaking. He must get a hold on himself.

Joslin tossed most of the night (he would have done better sleeping in front of the Aquarium entrance) and he was there with the help the next morning. An hour later the manager showed up.

The two men entered a small room. On a table in a crate the twelve from Florida waited. As the men approached they heard a chorus that any lover of the horny ones would have flipped over.

"Most unusual, Mr. Joslin. When you didn't arrive last night, I came in to see how the *Bufos* were doing. Doing? They were talking as though they were natives of California. Quite happy about the trip and their present quarters. Most of the amphibians of the genus *Bufo* and the family *Bufonidae* take time to adjust to such a terrific change as that between Florida and California. I guess, they feel there isn't such a difference after all. The Chambers of Commerce wouldn't like that, I'll wager."

The manager laughed. Joslin picked up the crate and headed for his car. As he entered the street crowded with traffic his thoughts soared. Maybe he'd win an Academy Award for Special Effects with these delightful little critters.

In the bare confines of his Paramount recording studio Joslin and his cortege of assistants watched the toads explore the setting he had prepared for them—a perfect replica of a Florida swamp!

One, two, three hours passed. Not a sound. Not even a yaup. Slowly on the fourth hour they began doing what toads do in a swamp. But they didn't croak, bawl or even plaint. One or two hopped. The rest just sat and blinked.

Hearing his heart plopping, Joslin mistook it for croaking and switched on his network of recording equipment. When an assistant reminded him of the silence emitting from the swamp, he switched it off, red-faced.

What to do?

"I can't understand it, Mr. Joslin. As I told you they croaked not more than ten minutes after arrival. It's hard to tell. Maybe they just like the atmosphere of the Hollywood Aquarium. You know, we try to please all species."

Joslin was sweating.

"Maybe if I brought them back to your place they'd croak again. Could I record there?"

"You're most welcome, Mr. Joslin. But what about the other sounds there? We have 10 dogs, 30 puppies, 60 lovebirds, 135 canaries, 13 parrots, 49 monkeys, 1 pony, 8 ducks, 2 geese, 54 rabbits (which don't say too much), 5 goats, 16 waltzing mice, 5 squirrels (who make quite a racket in their wheels). How can we muffle them?"

"With your permission and a handsome bonus, we can move them!"

Joslin listened to his heart plopping again.

"Since this is a De Mille special, I am sure I can cut red-tape—with the help of your bonus. When can I expect you?"

Two moving vans emptied the Aquarium in an hour and transplanted the menagerie to the Paramount property department.

Since outside noises would mar the proceedings, Joslin, with the cooperation of the Hollywood Police Department, had an officer posted outside to halt traffic while the toads were talking and he was recording.

The manager had suggested he record in total darkness. So in that total darkness, Joslin and crew, with only pin-point lighting and faint dials to guide their labors, waited.

"Eight . . . nine . . . ten . . ." someone quipped . . . "Maybe toads only talk at midnight . . ." He wasn't far off. At exactly five minutes to the witching hour, the toads talked.

For two hours Joslin recorded the varying keys in the *Bufo* vocabulary. Exhausted and ecstatic Joslin packed up his equipment and dismissed the crew.

But a puzzlement: why did the toads only talk here?

He surveyed the room—nothing unusual, bare white walls and one window. Then he listened—the clock on the wall. Could be. His technical mind demanded to know. He shut off the clock. The toads stopped talking. He plugged it in again. The toads talked again. Incredible! But why had they waited so long? The clock had been there all through those hours. Well, forget it. He had them on record now and forever.

De Mille was so impressed listening to the toads he exulted:

"I'll have Paulette and Bob do the whole scene with the toad background. Maybe their tones will inspire a new kind of film lovemaking!"

38 RHUBARB

Temperament, melodramatics and walking off movie sets have ruined as many stars as scandal, the bottle and a stay in the pokey. But there have been exceptions where these transgressions paid off and the public forgave and grew to love the offenders. Among the animals who followed this path to stardom was Rhubarb, the cat.

He was disliked even by his trainer, Frank Inn, the most noted "cat man" in cinema city. Claw-marks on his hands and arms proved that many times a little strong-arming was employed by both members of the team.

But Rhubarb was the most famous cat in the world and even Inn had to make allowances.

It all began when Rhubarb was known as "Orangey," a doubtful member of the amazing feline stable run by Inn, who could supply a variety of cats to fit any situation or any plot.

As Frank described his purring brood:

"I have 'crate cats' which are raised in a crate and are trained to run back into it. When a scene in a movie requires a cat to run up a stairway, or through a room, all I do is place a crate in the right place and the 'crate cat' will always head for that spot.

"Then I have 'hunchback cats.' These are trained to hunch their backs for scenes involving mystery and haunted houses.

"My 'fraidy cats' will do 'scared runs' with their hair bristling, or cringe in a corner.

"A difficult cat to train is the 'shoulder cat.' This one will perch on a human's shoulder and stay put until he is yanked off.

"Among the other types are the 'yawning cats,' 'whisker-licking cats,' 'rug pulling cats,' which are used exclusively with children. But regardless of what type they are, they'll follow instructions only if they want to."

Because the fourteen-pound alleyer, Orangey, was the "I'll act when I want to" type, he won the greatest acting role ever written for a cat, the lead in H. Allen Smith's best seller, *Rhubarb*, in which a feline becomes the owner of the Brooklyn Dodgers.

"Foul-tempered, scar-faced sourpuss," that's what the script said

Rhubarb manages to upstage Ray Milland.

and out of hundreds of purrers testing for the difficult role, Orangey walked before the camera and, spitting at everyone, walked off with the part.

As the world's top paid kitty, on his first day of work, he pulled a runaway. Frank was not taken off guard. He *knew* his cats and could cope with them no matter what their temperament. He stationed dogs at every stage exit and the next time Orangey tried a getaway, he soon backed up, returned to the front of the camera, and began again to display his extraordinary talent.

Ray Milland was Rhubarb's co-star. The Paramount publicity department had changed his name for good or bad. Rhuby took a quick dislike to Mr. Milland. Maybe it was professional jealousy— after all, Mr. Milland had an Academy Award on his mantle. No one ever knew why for sure—not even Inn. "That's the trouble with cats," he sighed. "You never know why they do anything."

But Inn would not be outdone by Rhubarb. To outwhisker him he overcame his dislike for Milland by smearing liver paste on the actor's hands, so when Rhuby had to do a scene in which he was required to display affection for his master, he quickly—and at least outwardly—kiss-licked his hands. But when Rhuby's taste for liver paste waned and he turned his tail up in Milland's face, catnip was substituted and he lovingly caressed the back of Milland's neck or rubbed against his leg.

Walter O'Malley may not know it, but here's the real owner of the Dodgers.

Rhubarb is chaffeured by his canine friend, Cleo.

Frank explained this way to a cat's stomach even when he doesn't want to earn his hundred dollars a day.

"A cat becomes lazy and spoiled if it's served only one type of food. The best cats for films are gluttonous ones, because they learn to perform for their food. I don't feed this type the day before they work. But after they are through with their scene they can have anything and everything they want.

"Cats are absolutely commercial. They won't work for a pet or an ear rub like other animals. They always have a paw out for a payoff after doing their stint. If the tidbit isn't there, you get a baleful stare, and you can be sure that all the coaxing in the world won't get that cat to do the trick again. You can fool a lot of people a lot of times, but you can fool a cat—just once."

But as Rhubarb's cat-antrums threatened the completion of the film, Frank was summoned to a conference. When asked what was wrong with the tabby, he shook his head. "A cat's a cat and everyone of them has a different nature. You can't ask Rhuby to be twenty-two cats." An executive producer jumped to his feet: "Then get twenty-two cats!"

So Rhubarb again topped all animal stars. He had twenty-two doubles and stand-ins for any emergency that arose due to his indisposition or cussedness.

Preview audiences applauded *Rhubarb* to the last whisk of its star's tail. The film was a hit and the world's meanest cat became its most loved.

An interesting footnote. Lloyds of London insured Rhubarb for the run of the film and made it all legal in this manner: Rhubarb's paw print, photo and a sound track of his voice were attached to the end of the policy for identification purposes.

Furor always followed the once-named Orangey. While acting with Jackie Gleason on location in Paris for *Gigot,* writer Pierre Galante of *Paris Match,* was commissioned to do a book titled *The Memoirs of Rhubarb.* But H. Allen Smith, creator of Rhubarb, threatened a lawsuit claiming "that cat made more money than I did out of the picture and he's not getting another red cent out of my brainchild."

Frank Inn commented:

"My cat is an actor, the best in the world, can play any part. Of course I don't own the name *Rhubarb.* So maybe we'll go back to Orangey."

It didn't matter much since Orangey roamed the Hollywood star dust trail as Minerva in the TV series, *Our Miss Brooks* and won himself a Patsy Award as just Cat, co-starring with Audrey Hepburn, in *Breakfast at Tiffany's.*

Maybe sage Shakespeare's advice in *Romeo and Juliet* answers the dilemma:

"What's in a name?"

39 HOW LASSIE CAME HOME

"The cat will mew and the dog will have his day . . ."

Shakespeare foretold it 400 years ago and a golden collie made it come true in 1941. And this is how he came home with a fortune and a new name.

"He chases cars and motorcycles, chews up everything in the house and the yard, barks constantly when we're not home, is eight months old and not housebroken. Do you think you can do anything with him?"

Rudd Weatherwax watched the beautiful collie pup scampering around the yard, inspecting the empty kennels, barking at the family cat.

"What's his name?"

"We call him Pal."

As the pup jumped up on Rudd: "Let me have him for a week."

The Weatherwax brothers, Rudd and Frank, had their first client and Frank had just finished painting the sign over their North Hollywood home, which read: STUDIO DOG TRAINING SCHOOL.

In the seven days that followed Rudd corrected most of Pal's bad habits and discovered the pup had extraordinary talent that set him to wondering about his future.

His future was decided when Pal's owner returned and told him the family had never enjoyed such peace and quiet and would he keep the pup for the training and board fees.

The bill came to ten dollars and the Weatherwaxes needed it. As Pal licked his hand he heard himself answering without thinking: "It's a deal."

Walking back into the yard Rudd remembered the often repeated admonition of producers—"Collies are too high strung for motion pictures." But he also remembered Jean, the first dog star, was a collie.

Almost a year passed, in which Pal developed beyond Rudd's highest hopes. He learned more than twenty-five tricks in the first six months. Of the forty dogs now in training Pal was tops and yet when taken on a studio call he was never chosen for even a "bit" role.

Liz Taylor was the *human* star of *Courage of Lassie*.

Was Pal going to be just a pal despite his terrific talent?

Loved by everyone who knew him, one day a friend of Rudd's suggested he let him take the dog for a few days' vacation on his ranch. The training had been strenuous and Rudd felt Pal needed the change of pace. It was the beginning of a strange turn of events.

Three days later Rudd read in a movie column that M.G.M. had bought the 1940 best seller, *Lassie Come Home*, by Eric Knight. Dogs were being auditioned for the starring role. Collie dogs! As his family crowded around him Rudd predicated Pal's day had come.

He drove at high speed out to his friend's ranch. Excitedly both men rushed on to the hillside. His friend called long and loud. Suddenly Pal bounded out of the brush. When Rudd whistled he came like lightning, and when Rudd saw him he felt he had been struck by it. Pal was a mass of burrs. His silken ruff was shredded from chasing rabbits. He looked like he'd been through a Marine obstacle course twice.

Back home the family stood around as if at a wake. Suddenly Rudd pounded his fist.

"I'm still going to take him to that audition. He was born for that part of Lassie!"

After much bathing and combing, combing and bathing, Pal still looked like a rag dog.

Rudd looking Pal in the eyes.

"You can act the part and with a little time you'll look it. I've just got to take you out to that audition, you know that, don't you, boy?"

Pal smiled his approval.

At the Hollywood Stars' ball park, where the auditions were being held, 300 dogs were put through their traces. As the talent scouts passed Pal they didn't even look at him. None of the dogs were chosen. The field was narrowed to twelve. But Rudd patted Pal's head:

"You'll play Lassie. I know it!"

For six months trainer and dog were inseparable. When another item in a local newspaper stated M.G.M. was still looking for a Lassie, Rudd telephoned the studio and was given an appointment for the following day. Again man and dog stormed the walls of the lion.

Ushered into the office of director Fred M. Wilcox, Pal took charge of the moment. He looked at Wilcox. Wilcox looked at him. He walked over and extended his paw as if he had known him all his

Lassie, now a TV star, drifts along with Jon Provost.

life. The director smiled and asked Rudd to have Pal perform a few tricks.

Pal was perfect.

"Let's see our producer Sam Marx."

After a second routine the smiling Marx said:

"I think we'd better make a film test of Pal. How about tomorrow morning?"

Pal had never worked before a camera and crew and Rudd wondered whether the strange atmosphere might shake him up. Rudd could have spared himself the worry. The collie followed Rudd's instructions to the letter and acted like a veteran.

The next day, following the run of the test, Rudd and Pal signed the contract of their lives. For publicity purposes Pal put his paw on a piece of paper held up by a fetching starlet. It was a rare moment for the "dog that wasn't wanted."

And then began the search for a boy to play opposite the dog.

It almost ended before it began. M.G.M. was so convinced that Roddy McDowall was the only youngster in filmland for the role that the company shot around him for two months while waiting for him to complete another assignment.

Roddy and Pal never let M.G.M. down on one foot of film. The picture was a hit and the saga had begun.

In an exciting sequence in which Lassie swims the Tweed River that divides England and Scotland (the scene was filmed in California's San Joaquin River) Lassie proved he was a born actor.

As Rudd Weatherwax recalled the memorable moment:

"Two boats were used with two cameras in one. I had Pal in the other. As director Wilcox shouted: Camera! Action! I commanded Pal to jump in the river. While he swam by the camera-boat I was rowed back to shore where I waited for him to come out some fifty feet away.

"Slowly he dragged out of the water, it was supposed to be a long swim, and as I directed him he slumped on the bank, dropped his head on the ground, stretched his paws and closed his eyes in weary exhaustion. Even the crew got choked up.

"Later Wilcox said to me: 'Pal jumped in the water, Rudd, but Lassie climbed out.'"

When the picture was previewed many praises were heaped on the beautiful collie but the one that stuck most was a critic's imaginative comment: "He's a Greer Garson in furs."

With success ringing in his ears Lassie proceeded to follow in the footsteps of M.G.M.'s roster of two-legged stars.

He began with a unique first, *The Lassie Radio Show,* on a national network. The series featured a dramatic story of a dog, with Lassie barking, growling and whining through a script that didn't have a word in it—for him.

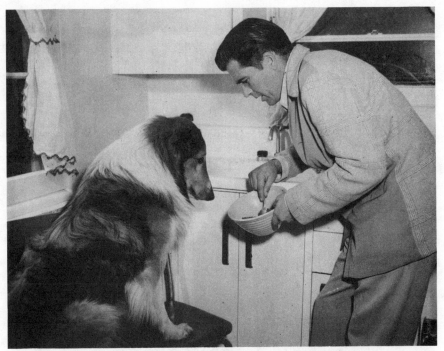

Rudd Weatherwax serves Lassie breakfast.

Lassie carries a message in *Courage of Lassie*.

Marquise and Lassie talk things over.

His personal appearances throughout the country were always SRO and earned him checks as high as a thousand dollars a performance. He enjoyed the luxury of his own private compartment during train-travel, and had a station wagon to transport him to and from the theater.

Lassie's popularity rose like a balloon that every man, woman and child in America had a string attached to.

But this acclaim and adoration sometimes had its moments of panic and even danger.

A handful of youngsters watched intently as scenes for *Son of Lassie* were being filmed at the North Hollywood Park. During a lull they gathered around the dog star, petting and asking him questions, just as they would have with any human star. Director S. Sylvan Simon called Rudd over to discuss a difficult scene, which left Lassie alone with his rabid fans.

A few minutes later as Rudd started back to the little group he went wild-eyed as he saw several boys armed with scissors, clipping locks of hair from Lassie's coat.

Rushing in he grabbed the scissors with his first panic-stricken breath and shouted reprimands after taking his second one. As he looked at the long faces he tried to make the seriousness a little light-hearted.

"Say, are you fellows trying to finish Lassie's career? He's not old enough yet to play bald-headed parts."

Lassie and Roddy McDowall.

One of the kids quipped back: "Gee, Mr. Weatherwax, we can trade one lock of Lassie's hair for three autographed Lana Turner pictures! Ain't that worth trying for?"

Lassie received thousands of fan letters but one that came from Togo, a Dalmatian guard dog on MP duty at Fort McPherson in Georgia, topped them all. It seems a pin-up of the beautiful collie hung on the wall of Togo's army kennel. Obviously Togo didn't know the ways of Hollywood and that Lassie was a male.

As Brownie, the Chaplin dog, helped to start the career of Baby Peggy in the early Twenties, Lassie, in the Forties, extended a paw to another star-to-be—Elizabeth Taylor.

A little girl had been hired to play a wee Scot in the *Courage of Lassie*. But as she appeared before the camera she squinted constantly. Finally it was discovered the bright lights were too much for her weak eyes. She had to be replaced.

When writer-producer Edgar Selwyn overheard Sam Marx and Fred Wilcox discussing the problem over luncheon in the M.G.M. commissary, he told them that he had just the girl. Sara Taylor, an English actress, had just arrived from London with her ten year old daughter, Elizabeth, to escape the Nazi blitz. Elizabeth was incredibly beautiful—and talented.

On the set the men stared at the little girl walking toward them. Even the warm afternoon air seemed cooled by her grace, her raven black hair, and the lustre of her violet tinted eyes.

She introduced herself, did a little curtsy and asked the gentlemen if they would like to see her do a dance she had done for the Princesses, Elizabeth and Margaret Rose. They replied they would. Entranced they watched and with the gentle, feather-like movements of a fairy princess, Elizabeth Taylor reached out and captured their hearts.

At the finish, Lassie, unprompted, went over and kissed the little girl on the cheek.

The capacity for a dog to love a man, to seemingly understand his problems and share his darkest moments have been told again and again. But Lassie's great heart will long be remembered in an Army hospital in Vancouver, Canada, where the redoubtable star was appearing. A crowded and exhausting day had seen him performing from early morning to nightfall. But at the end of the gruelling routines the collie gave his greatest performance on a flat-topped truck.

As Rudd watched him he could hardly believe his eyes. But he knew his wonderful Pal was capable of many strange and inspiring acts.

Following the show they made the rounds of the wards of the bed-ridden patients. Time was precious so Lassie stopped only briefly. In one bed an old man smiled at the dog, who halted, and without even turning to Rudd for permission walked over to the bed, sort of bowed, and squatting on his hindquarters placed both paws on the covers. The old man smiled again, and with difficulty, reached out and patted his head. Slowly tears welled up in the old man's eyes, in the dog's eyes, in every eye on the ward.

As the nurse came up Rudd asked if it was all right to let Lassie spend a little time with the old gentleman. She nodded sadly.

"Yes, Mr. Weatherwax. He has very little time left."

Why did Lassie give the old soldier his special attention? Did he sense the nearness of death? How did he know . . . ?

The Lassie series lasted almost ten years which is a record in the annals of animal-starring movies. In 1952 came the final fade-out and M.G.M., to settle their contract with Weatherwax, allowed him to keep the name Lassie.

Was the dog star setting?

Robert Maxwell, producer of Superman thought otherwise. Sometime later he signed a contract with Weatherwax for a TV series which called for Lassie's salary at $1500 a show and 10 per cent of the profits.

The rest is small screen history.

Strangely enough the original Lassie never appeared on TV. A son sired by Pal romped across the flickering box to the delight of millions. And critics and competitors have pondered the continuing success of the Lassie dynasty; there have been four of them.

It's quite simple. He is everybody's dog. Even to those who don't like dogs. There just always has to be a Lassie because the heart of America would miss a beat without him . . .

40 TOO MANY OATS

In 1950 Francis was the most famous mule around the globe and just a step behind Lassie in popularity. Teamed with Donald O'Connor he made people in every land laugh because he had a man's voice.

Preparing *Francis Goes to the Races,* the men in charge of producing pictures at Universal-International studios sent for Jimmy Phillips, the mule star's trainer.

They told him they had heard stories that Francis was 250 pounds overweight. Didn't he know a star of Francis's fame had to watch pounds like a human?

Jimmy, who loved Francis like a brother, tried to explain:

"The trouble is that Francis has just been standing around for almost a year since his last movie. Mules can't do that. And if you had a back and a bottom like Francis you'd see how oats go to fat when they aren't exercised."

None of the men laughed.

"We'd never have had this weight problem if Francis had worked. His two stand-ins that do rough scenes for him worked in other movies as extras and are nice and slender. When I saw Francis gaining I suggested to you gentlemen that he do a little extra work. But you said, 'Francis is a valuable star. What would happen to his box-office draw if he appeared as an extra?' So he just kept standing around."

The head men looked at each other and then one said:

"You either take 250 pounds off Francis or he goes to pasture!"

Later that day Jimmy told Francis what the head men had said. Jimmy and Francis did talk to each other—but not like on film—with a man faking his voice. They talked with their eyes and the lines in their faces and a nod of the head.

Francis said he'd do anything Jimmy wanted. He didn't like being a fatty himself. Jimmy hugged his neck and pulled his ears and told him to be ready bright and early the next morning for a workout.

Francis' first exercise was to keep up with Jimmy's station wagon.

Donald O'Connor, Martha Hyer, and *Francis in the Navy*.

Tied to the rear, Jimmy drove Francis around the Hollywood hills at speeds up to 15 miles an hour. After an exhausting week with people staring at the duo as if they were out of their minds, Francis lost 100 pounds.

Jimmy cut down on Francis's feed. Instead of oat hay he let Francis munch on alfalfa, which was watery and less fattening.

He also had a special steam cabinet built. In this contraption the cooperative mule sweated off another fifty pounds.

But still his rump was too big and he walked too hippy for the cameras from any angle. Jimmy and Francis went back to driving around the Hollywood hills. At the end of another week Francis had hardened up his flabby muscles and looked a lot trimmer, but he hadn't lost a pound.

Francis Goes to the Races was ready to go before the cameras. Was Francis?

The morning Jimmy reported back to the head men he parked Francis outside the conference room. Francis tried to look funny so Jimmy would go in with a smile on his face, but Francis looked sadder than Jimmy.

Francis delivers his acceptance speech after winning the first Patsy Award, 1951.

The "duck" is out of gas, so Francis comes to the aid of Donald O'Connor.

Again the question was put to Jimmy. He braced himself and remembered all the deeds mules had done throughout history and called on their courage to ride out this crisis.

"Gentlemen, when I told Francis what you said he eagerly cooperated. I never saw a mule work so hard and try so hard. We've done everything. Ran over hills, dieted and even I had a steam cabinet built for him."

One of the head men laughed.

"That cabinet was good for a lot of publicity. Imagine, a mule in a steam bath!"

No one else laughed.

"Well, gentlemen, we've tried, I tell you, we've tried. But I guess we can't make the weight you asked. Francis is shy 50 pounds."

Slowly the door pushed open. Francis poked his head into the conference room. The head men stared at Francis. Francis stared back: eyes tearful . . . pretended smile . . . . ears drooping almost to his chin. . . .

Suddenly the man who had laughed stood up and walking over to Francis patted his sides and said:

"What's fifty pounds more or less to a mule? Francis is a star and he can overcome a little handicap like that."

Picking up his Patsy Award, Francis agreed with the head man. Only in Hollywood could it happen to a mule.

41 THE DISNEY DOGS

A mouse first marched at the head of the Disney parade, but first in cartoon and now in living hair, the dogs have taken over for the maker of the most human motion pictures anywhere.

From Pluto of the flopping ears and flopping ways to the canines of *Lady and the Tramp* and *One Hundred and one Dalmatians*, man's best friend came out of inkwells instead of kennels and back alleys.

But with such hits as *The Shaggy Dog, Greyfriars' Bobby, Old Yeller, Big Red* and *Savage Sam*, the Disney factory has just gone to the real dogs.

What dogs!

Sammy's Shadow, owned by Mrs. Addie Anderson of Rialto, California, a pedigreed thoroughbred sired by Ch. Norval Pride King—at the time the top Old English Sheep Dog in the United States—out of Ch. Lillibrad Lindy Lou, had no movie aspirations. But when the Disney scouts saw him working out in an obedience-training school, they signed the mop-pawed, hairy-eyed clown to test for the lead in *The Shaggy Dog*.

As director Charles Barton viewed the result he smiled: "He's a natural-born Disney character if I ever saw one. He'd make a statue laugh."

Shaggy, name-changed, was the only canine to play a human being in motion pictures—a teen-age boy who had been turned part-time into a Bratislavian sheep dog. Critics wrote: "It was hard to tell when the boy and the dog were separated." Shaggy proved the critics were right by winning the Tenth Annual Patsy Award for 1960's best performing animal star in the movies.

One hundred years ago the true-life story of a little terrier, a descendant from the Isle of Skye, who mourned at his master's grave for fourteen years, touched the hearts of the world.

Walt Disney, reading its retelling in *Greyfriars' Bobby*, swallowed the lump in his throat and sent his talent scouts scurrying to Scotland to find a ball of fur the size of a lady's muff to recreate the classic.

A "Shaggy Dog" scene, with Shaggy and Kevin Corcoran. (C MCMLIX Walt Disney Productions)

Roaming the streets of Chorley, in Northern Scotland, they found the living image: his name, Tam O'Shanter.

Tammy, as the four-footed tyke of *Greyfriars' Bobby,* again touched the hearts of the world. But great parts don't come along every day in Hollywood. So Tammy, rather than do bit roles or walk-ons, decided to pack up his biscuits and head for his homeland.

Will Tammy ever return?

His mistress, who saved him from the streets for twelve shillings ($1.44) says, "If the right role comes up Tammy will always be ready to go before the cameras. But now, he enjoys visiting with the townspeople and watching his favorite television programs." How happy can a doggie be?

Bobby greets Andrew Cruickshank in this scene from *Greyfrairs Bobby*. (C Walt Disney Productions)

The schedule for *Big Red* outlined a most ambitious outdoor adventure epic. Not since the days of Rin Tin Tin would an animal enact such a demanding character. But Walt Disney didn't send out a rush call for a dog; he picked up the phone and called one of the best canine experts in cinemaland—Bill Koehler.

Bill had worked on *Shaggy Dog* and *Swiss Family Robinson*. He was the one man to come up with an Irish Setter who could play Redcoat Reilly of Wintapi: Red Coat, who must hunt, run and jump; Redcoat, who must endure taxing water sequences; Redcoat, who must obey on a single command in the most intimate of scenes.

There was no precedent. No Irish Setter had ever acted such a part. But Bill didn't say no to anything.

After four months of screening prize Reddies, Koehler chose Champion Red-Aye Scraps, U.D. (Utility Dog—the utmost in obedience), trained and bred by Larry and Eleanor Heist of Ontario, California.

The Irish Setter had no acting experience. He had never appeared before a camera. His first day was a severe test to his sensitivity and obedience.

In the scene Scraps takes the hand of the boy star (Gilles Payant) in his mouth and gently leads the runaway across a field to Walter

The sign tells the story of *Greyfrairs Bobby*. (C Walt Disney Productions)

Pidgeon. A tender and difficult routine, Scraps did it in less than an hour. As the camera came in for a head close-up, he *was* Big Red.

In 1963, along with the Academy Awards won by the Disney pictures, Big Red brought home the Patsy Award as the best in his field.

"It was about four years ago, at the Van Nuys dog pound, that I noticed Spike," Rudd Weatherwax, owner and trainer of Lassie, recalled. "He was just a pup, but he looked smart. I thought he might make an actor, so I bailed him out for three dollars."

Star of *Old Yeller,* the lop-eared, 115-pound mutt, as a weather-beaten range dog who helped protect a pioneer homestead in frontier Texas, proved that glamor and good looks weren't everything an actor needed in Hollywood.

**Red Coat Reilly of Wintapi, as *Big Red*, welcomes Gilles Payant home.
(C MCMLXI Walt Disney Productions)**

Fighting bears, a wolf and a pack of wild hogs, Spike came pretty close to being a John Wayne on four legs.

Weatherwax continued to discuss his rugged celebrity: "He does everything but talk and darned if I don't think he might do that if someone wrote proper dialogue for him."

Spike lived in the lap of luxury, contrary to his rough-hewn appearance, and was chauffeured to the studio in a station wagon equipped with a chromium-plated cage. On the sound stage his dog house was heated in the winter and cooled in the summer. He ate constantly and sometimes demanded extra nourishment for a strenuous scene.

All Spike wants now is to play opposite John Wayne and settle the arguments over their talents once and for all.

"The first time we saw him," trainers Bill Koehler and Hal Driscoll said, "he seemed so forlorn looking, with his head hanging down and his ears like they had weights in them, we both decided to call him 'Tom Dooley' after the famous songs, 'Hang Down Your Head, Tom Dooley.' "

The transformation from a hang-dog mutt to the tough-as-leather tracker of renegade Indians who have kidnapped his young master was quite a leap. But Tom Dooley did it in *Savage Sam*.

Skirmishes with wolves, cornering a bobcat, riding a horse and attacking Apaches put Dooley on the roster alongside such great westerners of silent and sound movies as William S. Hart, Tom Mix and Hoot Gibson.

The chase, the fight and the kill were his meat. The only problem would arise after the camera stopped grinding: Dooley, a good

Kevin Corcoran goes for a dip with Spike in *Old Yeller*. (C MCMLVII Walt Disney Productions)

Brian Keith and Tommy Kirk, with animal star in *Savage Sam*. (C MCMLXII Walt Disney Productions)

hound dog, wouldn't stop the action despite cries from his trainers.

What to do? To save production costs and time Dooley was allowed to track out his hot trail in order to satisfy his hound instincts. No other star can say he's had such a privilege.

So the Disney dogs romp across the movie and television screens all over the world. But any dogs reading these success stories had better bone up on some advice from Tammy of Scotland.

"It was great fun and the money certainly comes in handy. Save it while you got it—every coin of it. Who knows? If I'd had a couple of failures, with living costs in Hollywood and taxes, I might have ended up back on the streets. Watch even your shillings, laddies, and you'll always have a biscuit with your spot of tea . . ."

42 THE DISNEY WILD ANIMALS

All film fans know that Walt Disney's first love was Mickey Mouse, Donald Duck, Pluto and dozens of furry and feathered fellows that delighted his short and feature movies. But Walt also had a second love—a love of nature and its creatures. For years he nursed this desire to capture on celluloid the animals in their own world without hindrance of Hollywood hokum.

Documentary films under such inspired cinema poets as Robert Flaherty and Paul Rotha had reached art form status. So in 1947 with 20 years hard experience behind him, Disney ventured into the wildlife drama.

Some predicted instant failure. All were surprised when instant success marked this bold program.

Disney first told his associates their initial purpose was to entertain. They must make audiences enjoy and thrill to the real life drama of nature's creatures. They must not teach. But strangely enough as the pictures evolved nature outlined her own truths and laws and those seeking to probe its mysteries found invaluable information and knowledge never previously shown on the silver screen.

He assigned individual cameramen to projects and photographic teams to others. They had sole responsibility for their product. They trained their lenses on mother nature and watched and waited and wondered.

Stories were developed but along only the most researched lines possible. They were never to digress for semi-dramatic effect an inch from nature's own plan.

Time and money were to be freely spent. Disney asked only for the living result. And the result was astonishing. Audiences found themselves involved with the ways of ants, lions and creatures with unpronounceable names as if they were next-door neighbors. They were swept up in the vibrating canvases of jungle, desert and white wilderness. They were awed by the struggle for survival and nature's handling of overpopulation. As they filed from packed theatres they all felt a little closer to the mystery and wonder of life itself.

The films following this instant success then emerged dynamically. There was more analysis of the protagonists and the films were more scientific. The public clamored and applauded. Applause also reached the Academy Awards ceremonies and the Oscars crowded into Walt Disney's office until he almost had to add another room. The final count was one hundred.

The first in the series was *Seal Island,* which won an Academy Award in 1949. Today it is still the world's most famous short subject. The fur seals are those amphibious and polygamous giant mammals which arrived in May at Pribiloff Islands in the Bering Sea off Alaska. They remain until fall. With an enormous colony of new born pups, they then set out for their winter migration.

Another water-dwelling animal, the furry flat-tailed and industrious beaver, starred in *Beaver Valley.* He lives in his own do-it-yourself pond, struggling continuously against his pesky neighbors—herons, frogs, woodchucks, and a few otters—who all use his pond for their own needs. This film short received the 1950 Academy Award and 14 other awards from other sources.

Nature's Half Acre, a third Academy Winner in 1951, gathered 11 different awards, which marked it as a masterpiece. This film required the extraordinary talents of 15 cameramen, as it showed the miracle of abundant life on a Midwestern plot of grassland. The area provides food to a dozen species of birds and another dozen kinds of insects, as well as many different plants—all of which contribute to the eternal balance of nature.

The Olympic Elk stumped Disney until he found the world's most famous naturalist-photographic team, Lois and Herb Crisler. For two years they braved alone all the dangers of life in the Washington State mountain range, searching out and photographing the annual trek of the last great herd of the Olympic Elk. This herd, stalked by wolves and other predators, moves from the lower rainforests up through the primeval mountains to the summer grazing meadows, high among the crags. Throughout the four seasons the Crislers immortalized this drama on celluloid.

The 1952 Academy Award winner was *Water Birds,* an exquisite and delicate tapestry portraying the grace and beauty of the birds, their rainbow plumage against the green waters and blue skies. Wild fowl of the seacoasts and marshlands are the stars.

Water birds have no song as such—merely cries, calls and the noisy beating of wings. So, a unique musical score brings the final dimension—a symphony to simulate the birdsong, with a tempo and rhythm to imitate the beat of the wings, the soaring in flight, and the feeding, courtship and nesting.

Lensed by the famous team of Alfred and Elma Milotte, who

Crouching lion is waiting for approaching band of impala to graze within charging distance in *The African Lion*. (C Walt Disney Productions)

A lioness and her cubs savor a meal, in *The African Lion*. (C Walt Disney Productions)

had photographed *Seal Island, Bear Country* takes place in the Rocky Mountains of Montana and Wyoming where the great American Black Bear, with his highly disciplined but happy and complex family live with its morals, obedience and intelligence. This picture was also a winner of Awards in 1952.

In 1953 two contrasting films made movie history—*Prowlers of the Everglades,* a swamp saga, and the True-Life Adventure's first full-length feature (and Academy Award winner), *The Living Desert.*

Both pictures explored areas of much mystery as patient skill and brilliant photography brought to light the infinite species of life abounding in both places. The alligator is the voracious and unchallenged monarch in *Prowlers of the Everglades.* He rules the skunks, otters, raccoons, birds and snakes within his reach yet all his natural prey become his enemies because the alligators' eggs and newborn babies are food for many animals and birds of the swamp. Underwater photography was used here and made a thrilling impact upon the audience.

In direct contrast, the first full-length feature, *The Living Desert,* proved that a desert is not a lifeless, desolate stretch of arid land, but is often overrun with plant life, tortoise, coatimundi, peccary, bobcat, snakes, hawks and many different insects and a variety of wildflowers. The picture carried off the '53 Academy statue and 16 other awards from all parts of the world.

Because of the spectacular response everywhere, Disney immediately ordered a second full-length feature for 1954. *The Vanishing Prairie* became the most panoramic, comprehensive and inclusive of all the adventures. It embraced the Great Central Plains, showing the sweeping skies, the mesas and the meadows with their teeming animal kingdom.

One of our national symbols, the American bison, the first of the vanishing wildlife of the prairie, grazes the rangeland. The chaos of these creatures as they swim through a flash flood and race before a raging fire started by lightning is spellbinding. And in the winter the numbing cold attacks the beasts as they forage for their lives.

Alfred and Elma Milotte, after three years in the African veldt, brought home one of the most engrossing studies—*The African Lion.* Lions and lionesses with their cubs stalk the herds of beautiful grazing zebra and the various antelopes such as the hartebeest and impala. The waterholes of the area, drawing every kind of creature, are a playground for the elephants, harmless unless angry or startled. The Milottes, at one point, endured their first fright when they found themselves captive in their lorry surrounded by some 400 elephants. But the pachyderms never raised a trunk at them. Other

Lioness brings home what's left of her kill, *The African Lion*. (C Walt Disney Productions)

A moose adds a light moment to *Beaver Valley*. (C Walt Disney Productions)

Scrounging for food, in *Bear Country* (C Walt Disney Productions)

Taking a rest, in *Bear Country*. (C Walt Disney Productions)

An owl stares fixedly into the camera in *Beaver Valley*. (C Walt Disney Productions)

In this scene from *Charlie the Lonesome Cougar*, the hero tries to stop the drift of a raft that he inadvertently released from its mooring. (C MCMLXVII Walt Disney Productions)

high points show the animals weathering a drought, dust storms, a plague of locusts and tropical rains until equilibrium returns to Nature. Six awards were picked up by this epic.

Secrets of Life in 1957, with 18 photographers and naturalists, explored further fascinations of Mother Nature. The pollination of fields of flowers and trees, the specialization of seeds in their formations so they can be borne by wind or birds, animals or people, to new areas where they sow themselves and soon replenish the earth.

Employing time-lapse photography for the first time, cameramen followed the life cycle and structure of the beehive and an ant colony. The camera stops at a common pond, peers through a microscope to watch the wriggly protozoa in a drop of pond water, discovering that some insects live off life in the pond and the pond fish live off the insects. On the seacoast the antics of the silly decorator crab, jellyfish, barnacles, kelp and grunion fish bring a laugh. The film ends climactically as a great volcano erupts and changes the surface of the globe.

Chico (left) meets a mate in *A Country Coyote Goes Hollywood.* (C
MCMLXIV Walt Disney Productions)

Photographer Dick Borden stands in a pit he dug himself to film a colony of black-footed Albatross in *Islands of the Sea*. (C Walt Disney Productions)

White Wilderness was number 12 in the series and ranged through the Canadian forests up into Alaska where the world's hardiest animals endure the world's worst climate, harsh and bitter cold. The arctic land and sea support large animals such as the polar bear, gray wolf, caribou, the vicious wolverine and the smaller but equally rugged fox and snowshoe rabbit and lemming.

The cold semi-frozen floes and seas of the North nourish the walrus and the seal, and two prehistoric creatures, the Beluga whale and the musk ox. Geese, gulls, falcons and cormorants abound on a diet of fish. One of the most scenic and popular, *White Wilderness*, garnered eight awards.

When it seemed that just about every approach to nature had been put on film, Disney came up with a wholly delightful exploration of life beneath the deep blue sea. In *Mysteries of the Deep*, he called some leading oceanographers away from their academic work to complete the project. Seven photographers explored the waters around Nassau and the Bahamas.

In 1959 the underwater camera techniques of lighting and filming in open water were still in their early stages of development, but the cameramen were so remarkable that they captured the fluid motion and color of the fish as they moved in their dark, deep-water world. In the ocean depths, eating and mobility are the first laws of survival, and managing not to be eaten is the next law of survival.

Revealed as another first are the vagaries of the octopus, the sea horse and the hermit crab who hides himself inside a snail shell after eating the snail. Three comedians of the deep, the barber shop shrimp, the French Angel fish and the Spanish hogfish, are all scavengers cleaning the barnacles and parasites from passing fish which come around to take advantage of their appetites. This enchanting adventure won two awards.

Flightless cormorants of the Galapagos Islands begin their time of nesting in this scene from *Islands of the Sea*. (C Walt Disney Productions)

Always on the alert watching for the dreaded skua gull, a predator who preys on young chicks, the adult rockhopper penguins of the Falkland Islands stand guard over their young, in this scene from *Islands of the Sea*.

A hermit crab (right) trespasses on a jawfish's territory and is quickly ordered off the premises in this scene from *Mysteries of the Deep*. (C Walt Disney Productions)

Bound for some dark and unknown destination, the moray eel glides across the ocean floor in *Mysteries of the Deep*. (C Walt Disney Productions)

Lobo, king of the wolves, is master of all he surveys in Disney's *Legend of Lobo*. (C MCMLXI Walt Disney Productions)

Closeup of a wolf spider, a fearsome desert creature. (*The Living Desert* C Walt Disney Productions)

"Old Yeller" fights off a bear that had threatened his master. (C Walt Disney Productions)

Coyotes eat roadrunners; but what do roadrunners enjoy for dinner? In this scene from *The Living Desert* a garter snake is evidently going to meet his fate. (C Walt Disney Productions)

Against a dense background of lush jungle plant life in the Amazon basin of Brazil, *The Jungle Cat,* or black jaguar, was filmed. Shown as the greatest hunter of all, in a life-and-death struggle the jaguar defends its tawny mate and the whole jungle against two mortal enemies—the crocodile and the boa constrictor. The monkey tribe rules the tree tops, along with the wily opossum, the sloth and the gayest, most colorful birds in any land—toucans, egrets, parrots and flamingoes.

Three cameramen and naturalists—James R. Simon, Hugh H. Wilmot and Lloyd Beebe—spent two years bringing back this fantastic footage. In 1960 it won two awards.

A culminating work of art in the natural science field was the production of *Perri,* a True-Life Adventure fantasy based on the children's classic by Felix Salten. The tale tells of a red pine squirrel named Perri who lives in a tall tree in Wildwood Heart in the mountains of Utah.

The contribution of the True-Life Adventure Series to man's understanding of wildlife is incalculable. For all time and generations to come these living canvases will inspire and awe long after the animals themselves have vanished from the earth.

What a fitting monument to the man most film fans consider Hollywood's greatest producer—Walt Disney.

A scene from *Jungle Cat*. Are the animals fighting or making love? (C Walt Disney Productions)

The Jungle cats in a friendly mood. (C Walt Disney Productions)

Four of *Nature's Strangest Creatures* (C Walt Disney Productions)

Koala

Tasmanian Devil

American Flying Squirrel

Spiny anteater

The baby alligators venture into a strange world for the first time in this scene from *Prowlers of the Everglades*. (C Walt Disney Productions)

A pair of ptarmigans meet up with a lemming (center) who has strayed from his herd in *White Wilderness*, Disney's feature about the strange patterns of survival among the creatures of the frozen north. (C Walt Disney Productions)

A polar bear catches a quick lunch in *White Wilderness*. (C Walt Disney Productions)

A red ant overcoming a black opponent in this scene from Disney's *Secrets of Life*. (C Walt Disney Productions)

Hayley Mills and friends in a scene from *The Moon Spinners.* (C MCMLXIII Walt Disney Productions)

Tommy Steele, playing a butler, grabs George, an eight-foot alligator, by the tail in a desperate attempt to steer the family pet back into the conservatory where he belongs. (The Happiest Millionaire C MCMLXVI Walt Disney Productions)

The homesteading prairie dog watches intently as a herd of wandering buffalo shuffles past his domain. (C Walt Disney Productions)

Ex-Mouseketeer Annette Funicello poses with friend in a scene from *The Misadventures of Merlin Jones*. (C MCMLXIII Walt Disney Productions)

43 THE MIRACLE OF THE DOLPHINS

By Ivan Tors

The Cinema's leading producer of animal films

All the great scientists, of past and present, who have placed man alone on top of the evolutionary scale should take a hard look at their findings. Somehow, they forgot the cetaceans, the family of whales and dolphins. Of course, this oversight is forgivable, as the first dolphin was trained only 13 years ago in Florida by Adolph Frohn and the first whale to be captured alive was taken seven years ago, by the Marineland of the Pacific.

To kill a dolphin or a whale, small or large, one day will be a crime similar to taking a human life. Cetaceans are not ordinary animals. They are creatures with large brains, like man. They love and protect their babies and depend on each other when in need. They never wage war—unlike man. They seem to have a language and are able to communicate with each other. When exposed to man, they try to emit human-like sounds in an attempt to communicate with him.

My first exposure to cetaceans was on the California coast. I observed many of the California grey whales on their yearly migrations from the Aleutians to Scammons lagoon in Mexico. When they passed my boat they appeared as friendly, curious creatures—neither afraid of man, nor afraid of the noise of our engines.

They approached us many times to take a good look at our boat. Their pinpoint navigation amazed me; they are capable of traveling—individually or in pairs—6200 miles to a rendezvous point without map or compass!

We were taking motion pictures of another species, the cunning killer whales. We observed them circling the sea lion and sea elephant islands. They would suddenly leap 20 feet out of the water, and then fall back on their sides with the sound of a cannon shot. The reflex reaction of sea elephants and sea lions to sudden noise is to take a nose dive into the water—in this case, only to become a tasty dinner plate for a hungry killer whale.

In another instance, when Frank and Boots Brocato from Marineland lassoed a 20-foot female killer whale, throwing a noose
from the 40-foot collecting boat, the lady was smart enough to wind
the line around the prop, immobilizing the boat, then to emit a
bloodcurdling distress call. Soon a 30-foot bull arrived to help the
lady in distress.

I have always admired the smaller dolphins for their skill and

**HAP'S CAP . . . falls into the water and becomes a toy for Flipper's
antics in the MGM-TV series' episode "Flipper's Bank Account."**

friendliness when they rode our bow waves with the speed of a tor-
pedo. . . . The original surf riders! Later on, I became better acquainted with them around the tanks of the Miami Seaquarium and
the Marineland of the Pacific. In captivity, they were friendly and
cooperative. They surpassed trained seals, dogs, and chimpanzees
in skill. Soon I realized that they were not like other animals—that
in certain areas of intelligence they even surpassed man.

My admiration for them developed further when I had a chance
to observe their gentleness. I was amazed at feeding time; no matter
how hungry they were or how they competed for fish or how fast
they grabbed it out of my hand with those long rows of 84 sharp,
threatening teeth, they never knicked or hurt me. They seemed to
be aware of their power and size and exercised the greatest caution
in their contact with a fragile 185-pound human.

"Clown"—one who weighed 450 pounds—used to jump seven
feet high, then take a lock of my hair between his sharp teeth and
tug it teasingly before falling back into the water. How "Clown"
knew just how much of a tug wouldn't hurt and how not to pull me
back with him into the tank is still a paradox to my inferior brain.

There is a familiar story told at Marineland. Some time ago
dolphins and moray eels lived together in peaceful coexistence in
the same tank. When one of the divers was bitten by a moray eel
while cleaning the bottom of the tank, one of the dolphins immediately grabbed the offending eel and threw it out of the tank. Here,
observing a new situation, the dolphin passed judgment, came to a
moral conclusion, and executed a sentence.

After falling in love with dolphins, I decided to make a movie
about them. When M.G.M. agreed to underwrite the cost, I began
to construct a wire fence around a coral reef in the Bahamas, where
my associates and I could work with dolphins in a natural environment. It was a new situation for man and the dolphin. In previous
experiments, man was out of the water while working with the
dolphin while the dolphin was inside a tank or enclosure. Now, all
of us were in the same element—swimming together, playing together—on a beautiful coral reef in 21 feet of water.

One of the dolphins we used was "Mitzi," a young 300-pound,
seven-foot-long female. She wasn't an oceanarium dolphin, but already had been exposed to people. She belonged to the Santinis from
Key Marathon, Florida. Mr. Santini was an expert in collecting
dolphins for oceanariums. He kept Mitzi as a pet, netting off a
lagoon from the ocean and keeping her there in considerable freedom. He visited her twice a day and fed her mullets.

Our other movie dolphins were never exposed to previous human
contact except when they were being caught. They were netted in
the ocean, transported to our coral reef, and placed in the ocean

THAT FANTASTIC FLIPPER . . . the title star of MGM's "Flipper's New Adventure," Flipper-the-dolphin, greets the human stars of the film, Luke Halpin and Pamela Franklin.

protected by our new fencing without any attempt at contact or training.

I cannot describe my surprise when I realized that the untrained bottle nosed dolphins fresh out of the ocean were even less hostile than the aquarium dolphins. Later on, all of this made good sense. Wild dolphins live in an environment of plenty. They are the fastest and strongest creatures. They can catch any fish they want. They don't have to be aggressive and compete for food while the oceanarium dolphins do.

I tested the aggressiveness of a large female dolphin by swimming toward her underwater and trying to grab her dorsal fin. All of my attempts at contact failed miserably as she swam away rapidly whenever I approached her. Once, I nearly succeeded, by cornering her at the shallow end against our fence. I watched her underwater through my face plate as she made her fast breakaway. Even in extreme panic, she never bared her teeth, and as she broke out made every effort to bypass me rather than to ram me.

This same unapproachable dolphin, a day after this experiment, became entangled in a net. In her desperate attempt to free herself she became more and more entangled. Coincidentally the famous dolphin scientist, Dr. John C. Lilly, was present. He immediately suggested that while I was trying to extract the dolphin from the net I keep stroking her. The dolphin never offered any resistance. She was completely paralyzed by fear and lay motionless in my arms. I lifted her above the waterline, so that her blow hole would be free of the water. On purpose, I extended the time of her disengagement to about ten or fifteen minutes while I kept stroking her with affection and talking to her in a gentle tone. Finally, she was free of her bonds, and I let her go. She swam away from me, but not in a panic! Her speed was moderate. Her attitude did not show any anxiety. I was able to pet her gently and hold her dorsal fin.

She didn't mind it. She kept towing me under and above water. Her transformation was quite miraculous. The next day she allowed my five-year-old son, Peter, to hop on her back and ride on her cowboy style clinging to the dorsal fin (just like in the ancient Greek legends; boy riding a dolphin).

This experience suggested to me that dolphins may not have to be tamed; that they are tame and gentle by nature; and that gentle

AT HOME . . . Flipper introduced Luke Halpin to his home beneath the sea as the two swim as a team in Metro-Goldwyn-Mayer's charming film, "Flipper." Produced by Ivan Tors the film stars Chuck Connors. James B. Clark directed.

DORSAL DERRING-DO! . . . Flipper's dorsal fin provides a perfect handle for his co-star in "Flipper's New Adventure," Luke Halpin. Luke merely grabs hold of the dolphin's fin, and the animal tows both the boy and an escaped convict to an underwater cave. There, the adventurous pair hold the desperado prisoner until help arrives.

physical contact by a human is enough to break the inter-species resistance.

It's quite possible that until a dolphin is touched by the human hand, he may think that we have shark-like, sandpaper-like skin which could hurt his extremely fine and silky skin. As soon as they become aware that our touch is no menace to them, and will not cause cuts or abrasions, they accept us as a friendly harmless species.

Many marine scientists warned me beforehand that I may encounter less gentle behavior from the male dolphins. Because of this warning, I was extremely cautious when I placed a young, untrained male into our ocean enclosure. To my great surprise, this male became similarly friendly. Of course, I have no way of knowing whether or not an older, more protective male would have behaved more aggressively.

Placing a female together with the male was a touching experience. They swam toward each other and touched flippers. It looked either like a kiss or handshake. They kept swimming together, touching each other every chance they had. Whenever they separated, they came together again in the form of a figure 8, touching flippers, kissing and swimming away.

Dolphins are, undoubtedly, sensual creatures—they like to touch and to be touched. Once we gained their confidence, they kept swimming to us, turning on their backs and permitting us to rub their bellies, backsides and flippers.

I heard from many experts that dolphins and sharks are deadly enemies and a dolphin is able to ram a shark to death. It is true that nearly all oceanarium dolphins carry remnants of shark bites. The Miami Seaquarium's famous albino dolphin, Snowball, has half of her dorsal fin bitten off.

One night, in the Bahamas, we captured a seven-foot Lemon shark. We placed the shark into our ocean enclosure with one of our seven-foot dolphins. We watched anxiously the behavior of the two creatures underwater. They did not fight at all, but it was obvious that there wouldn't have been any contest. The dolphin was so much faster, more alert and agile. She kept swimming circles around the much slower shark. It was a cat and mouse game without the dolphin ever trying to hurt the shark. The shark was afraid, and tried to hide on the bottom. The dolphin didn't like this, and immediately took a hold of the shark's tail fin to pull him up.

This was quite amazing: it was the basis for the many stories of dolphins saving shipwrecked sailors. Dolphins seem to be unhappy if anyone is close to a reef or stays on the bottom. Because of their own sensitive skins the proximity of any reef or bottom formation means danger to them. Often when my wife and children stood on the reef in the water, our dolphin kept upending them, trying to force them into a horizontal position—the natural position for any swimming creature. Besides, a dolphin is an air breathing mammal and must sound for air every two minutes. She probably was bothered by the fact that the shark kept hiding in the sand and not coming up for air.

This behavior contradicted the stories I heard about dolphins killing sharks by ramming them in their spinal cord or spleen, causing immediate death. Of course, our dolphin's friendliness toward the shark doesn't exclude the possibility that she would have attacked the beast had she mothered a baby dolphin.

The strength of the dolphin is prodigious. Experts in hydrodynamics still cannot understand or explain the phenomena of how the dolphin swims without causing any turbulence and how they are able to propel their 400 or 500 pound bodies at a speed of 30 or 40 miles per hour. Pedro, Miami Seaquarium's 550-pound dolphin, jumps as high as 20 feet with very little effort. When we trained Santini's Mitzi to pull a boat with my children in it, she pulled it effortlessly at a high speed.

When observing the fantastic physical attributes of these magnificent mammals, their gentleness became even more impressive. They didn't seem to enjoy killing. Although live fish is their natural food, immediately after we began feeding them frozen mullets, they stopped killing fish and depended completely on the diet provided by us.

I believe that dolphins have senses unknown to us. The first activity of our wild, male dolphin, after placing him in our enclosure, was to echo sound the reef and make a mental map. This was done in a very systematic fashion. He would turn toward each direction and emit a buzzing sound, which was audible to us underwater. It took him a good two hours to echo sound the reef. He would now know at all times—at night or in muddy waters—exactly where he was, and would be protected from bumping into dangerous obstructions. That this was the case was proved by a later experiment. Our enclosure was divided into two parts by a net. When we removed the net, our dolphin still would not pass through the non-existing line. Underwater formations or obstructions in the ocean do not change. A reef or a large rock will be there for thousands of years. Once it is mapped, it is accepted by dolphins as a fixed location. It is quite confusing for them to realize that men can move immovable objects. It often takes them days to readjust their maps and cross the imaginary lines of demarcation.

Later on, we placed a baby dolphin together with our female dolphin. One day I noticed with alarm our female dolphin lifting the baby toward the surface quite regularly. I had heard that sick dolphins would be supported this way by other dolphins. Our baby dolphin didn't show any signs of sickness or slowness. He kept swimming fast and furiously. To the casual observer, he did not look like anyone needing support. Unfortunately, the dolphin's instinct was more basic than our observations. The baby died three days later.

I noticed that the day before his death the other dolphin stopped supporting him. I learned later from other dolphin observers that this is quite natural. Once a dolphin knows that the sick dolphin is beyond the hope of recovery, the dolphin will stop the act of support. It certainly indicates great insight and extra-sensory capacities.

Just before the death of the baby, I gave penicillin injections to all our dolphins. When giving the shot into the muscle behind the dorsal fin, all dolphins seem to emit the same distress cry. Playing

FASTEST TUGBOAT UNDER THE SEA . . . Flipper the dolphin sticks her head into the loop of a rope and tows Luke Halpin's rowboat in this scene from MGM's "Flipper's New Adventure." The outboard motor runs out of gas and Flipper tows the boy to a deserted island.

this back to them underwater through an underwater speaker can cause attention and excitement among them.

I don't want to go into the field of communication of the dolphins, since this material has been extremely well covered in the book, *Man and Dolphin,* by Dr. Lilly. All I can do is testify that I heard dolphins, underwater, buzzing all new objects. I heard them whistling and crackling to each other underwater. In muddy water, I myself could follow them on the beam of the sounds they emitted. Above water, they tried to imitate our human vocalizations by whistling or a turkey gobble like sound. A striking example of their talent to imitate human noises was proven when our construction boss began to whistle on shore. Immediately, Mitzi surfaced and whistled back at him imitating his tone. This man, who had never been exposed to dolphins, looked incredulously at Mitzi, then kept

HAPPY TALK . . . Young Luke Halpin carries on a friendly conversation with his pet, the dynamic dolphin Flipper in this scene from the Metro-Goldwyn-Mayer production, "Flipper" which stars Chuck Connors and introduces Luke Halpin. Film was produced by Ivan Tors and directed by James B. Clark.

whistling. Mitzi kept whistling back. Having seen their impressive intelligence, it's not hard for me to believe that one day vocal communication between dolphin and man might be possible.

It was our observation that dolphins are one-shot learners. If we did have difficulty in any phase of training, it was because we weren't smart enough to communicate to them our intentions. Whenever we could make clear what we wanted they complied willingly and fast. For instance, Mitzi liked to retrieve things just like a dog bringing back the stick his master has thrown. The difference is that the dog always brings the object back in the same fashion. The dolphin is more sophisticated. When we threw Mitzi our swim fin she retrieved it the first time between her teeth. The second time, she balanced the fin on her nose. The third time, she carried it under her flipper the way a human would carry a briefcase under his arm.

It took us only a few hours to teach Mitzi how to tow a boat. We threw a noose with a float into the lagoon. Mitzi picked up the noose between her teeth and brought it back to us. We threw it out again. The second time, Mitzi placed her long beak into the noose and towed it back that way. We expressed our appreciation by patting her and throwing her her favorite fish. Immediately, she knew that this was the way we wanted her to bring back the noose. The next logical step was to tie the noose onto the line of a dinghy. Now, we threw the noose into the water attached to the dinghy, and Mitzi, without hesitation, towed the dinghy back to us full of children. She immediately realized our pleasure and appreciation, and from then on whenever the children threw in the boatline she automatically pushed her nose into the noose pulling the children.

Another time, I placed a net full of live fish into the enclosure. There were about 40 fish in the purse of the net. The bottom of the net was pursed together with a leadline, the top with a corkline. Mitzi surveyed the net without touching it. This, again, was different from any other animal behavior I have ever observed, as fish to her was like a banana to a monkey or a ham bone to a dog. Yet, she never touched the net—she didn't try to get to the fish either through a process of tugging or trial and error. She looked at the net, buzzed it with her sonar, then swam to the bottom of the net and picked up one of the lead weights between her teeth and pulled on it. This was the only way to get to the fish. Here was a completely new situation for her which she handled on the first try with logic and with results.

Then came the most amazing part of my observation. She let only one fish out, then dropped the lead weight back to its original position, thus keeping the other fish captive. She played with the free fish, but didn't eat it. She let it go, swam back to the net, and let a second fish out—again dropping the lead weight back into position to keep the rest of the fish captive. She ate the second fish. It was a Butter Fish, Mitzi's favorite. This went on all afternoon. She let the fish out, one by one, eating only Butter Fish and letting the others go.

This seems to be contradictory to what I said before about captive dolphins not killing live fish. In this respect, Mitzi was the same as the other dolphins, but we were forced to retrain her to feed on live fish, as in our motion picture we have a sequence where our dolphin has to catch and eat live mullets.

Someone could question the gentleness of the family of dolphins when the killer whale, which is a large dolphin, has been known to be the most ferocious of all living animals. This paradox puzzles me a great deal, and all I can say in the defense of these cetaceans is that there is no documented evidence that a human being has ever been attacked, unprovoked, by a killer whale. I talked to many skin divers who have seen killer whales while underwater and the killer whales passed by without attacking.

Others tell me that killer whales follow the great salmon migrations in the northern waters. They live on salmon almost exclusively. When, for certain reasons, salmon is scarce they become hungry fast. Their huge bodies burn up energy equivalent to 300 pounds of food a day. If no salmon is available, seals or dolphins might be the next most tasty morsel to appease their ravenous appetite. I respect their power and fearsome reputation, but I feel we need more evidence before calling them wanton killers.

Having worked with dolphins, I cannot escape thinking about the practical applications of their intelligence. As I just related, we taught Mitzi to bring us live fish out of the sea. I am convinced that they are much more efficient in fishing than we are and could be trained to chase fish into our nets. Some Everglades' fishermen told me how schools of dolphin surround schools of mullets. They swim around them in a tight circle, just like a purse seiner net surrounds a school. Then, only one dolphin will peel off and feed. After feeding, he will take his place again in the circle and let another dolphin peel off to feed. This kind of fishing calls for intelligence and a strong sense of cooperation.

I can see the time when we'll be riding dolphins in the water like cowboys ride their horses in the West. They could assist us in locating wrecks, laying cables, finding underwater ore deposits, towing boats, acting as life guards around beaches, keeping sharks away and guiding us to better fishing grounds.

In the next 20 years, we will hear and learn a lot about the dolphins, and they will learn a lot about us. My hope is that we won't disappoint them, and we'll behave just as kindly and gently towards them as they behave towards us.

44 FADE-OUT

In 1949, following the preview of the first "Francis" movie, at a studio conference a publicity man asked a simple question.

"Why don't we have Oscars for our animal actors?"

So almost forty years after Jean the Collie appeared in her Vitagraph series, awards were seriously considered for the animals.

Under the guidance of the American Humane Association, in cooperation with motion picture executives, the program swelled into a wave of enthusiasm and appreciation to recognize the achievements of the industry's so-called "dumb" actors.

On March 1, 1951, thousands of fans both inside and outside the Carthay Circle Theatre participated in the first Patsy Awards, with Ronald Reagan as master of ceremonies and presentations by James Stewart, Diana Lynn, Leo Carrillo and Rex Allen. Francis won the first Patsy.

After seven years, with the increasing importance of Television, the American Humane Association established an identical set of honors for animal actors appearing in this medium.

Patsy was an excellent choice for the award's name, since it meant either—Picture Animal Top Star of the Year or Performing Animal Television Star of the Year.

The awards are conducted by the AHA. Hundreds of entertainment editors, writers and critics are polled to determine the winner of the coveted first, second and third place Patsys in both media.

Additional awards of excellence are presented when the vote indicates deserving performances.

Another award, named in honor of the late Richard C. Craven, who established AHA's Hollywood office and pioneered an agreement with the MPAA Production Code to prevent cruelty to animals, is given to animals that ordinarily have no opportunity for a starring role, but excel in training, talent, ability and, of course, are humanely handled. This includes sustaining action and especially action such as falling, rearing, jumping and fighting. Past Craven

10th **ANNUAL PATSY AWARDS:** Shaggy, from Walt Disney's "The Shaggy Dog," "Picture Animal Top Star of the Year" and Asta, from the "Thin Man" series, "Performing Animal Television Star of the Year."

Awards include Jerry Brown, a "falling" horse; Smoky, a "fighting" stallion; Bracket, a "jumping" horse; Cocaine, a "falling" horse; and Sharkey, Dempsey, Choctaw and Joker, a four-up team that pulled stagecoaches and wagons across Western scapes for over ten years.

Both awards are only given when feature films and television programs meet AHA accepted standards.

The Second Annual Patsy Awards were also conducted at the Carthay Circle Theatre, featuring Susan Ball, Lex Barker, Arlene Dahl and Hugh O'Brian.

For the next three years, 1953–55, the presentations moved outdoors to the Devonshire Downs Fairgrounds at Northridge in San Fernando Valley. Chill Wills, noted character actor, and the "voice" of Francis, the Talking Mule, was master of ceremonies in '53 and '54, assisted by such glamor as Kim Novak and Pier Angeli. The 1955 Awards were highlighted by the live performance of famed stuntmen, trainers and animals.

11th ANNUAL PATSY AWARDS: Tramp, dog in "My Three Sons"
ABC/TV series with owner, trainer Frank Inn, "Performing Animal
Television Star of the Year" and King Cotton, horse in Columbia Pic-
tures' "Pepe," "Picture Animal Star of the Year" with owner-trainer
Ralph McCutcheon.

In 1956 the Patsy Trophies were handed out at each of the winning picture companies.

A chuck wagon luncheon spotlighted the Seventh Award ceremonies at the Glen Randall Training Ring in North Hollywood, attended by more than one hundred film industry representatives headed by James Garner, Patrick Wayne and Joanna Moore.

The 1958 Awards, for performances in '57, marked the introduction of Patsys for animals in Television, also presented at the Glen Randall Training Ring with more than two hundred stars, movie and TV executives, animal trainers and handlers in attendance.

The Ninth Award ceremonies took place at the Art Linkletter Playhouse in Hollywood with kids and animals having "their day." Young actors and actresses who presented and received awards included Jerry Mathers, Valentina Skelton, Tommy Nolan, Angela Cartwright, Johnny Crawford, David Ladd and Michael Winkelman. Dennis Weaver of *Gunsmoke* fame was master of ceremonies, and, for the first time, the achievement celebration was covered by both motion picture and television news cameras.

The Tenth Patsy marked another first—the ceremonies were nationally televised on more than 100 stations. Red Rowe acted as master of ceremonies filmed at CBS-TV in Hollywood. Young stars participating included: Jon Provost, Rusty Hamer, Ricky Kelma, Bobby Diamond, Richard Eyer, Noreen Corcoran, Annette Funicello, Tony Dow, Evelyn Rudie and Tammy Marihugh.

When the annual Academy of Motion Picture Arts and Sciences Awards moved their presentation ceremonies to the Santa Monica Civic Auditorium, Hollywood's famous RKO-Pantages Theatre became the home of the April Patsy functions.

Numbers 11, 12 and 13 have had unusual and far-reaching effects. While the AHA is in the National Federation of Societies for the Prevention of Cruelty to Animals, it also represents other humane organizations, many of which are concerned with children's welfare.

As a combined salute to kindness to animals and children the audience at the Pantages has been composed of less fortunate children selected by the Community Chest's Welfare Information Service.

Each year 1500 children thrill to seeing their favorite child and animal stars in person along with a major motion picture shown in advance of its world premiere.

A famous character actor watching the glow on the faces of the youthful audience adlibbed the final tribute to our animal actors:

"In the faces of children, when you can reflect joy, laughter and sometimes tears, in the faces of children you have played your finest hour whether before a camera or the Almighty, whether you are a man or an animal . . ."

12th ANNUAL PATSY AWARDS: (left to right) Rutherford T. Phil-
lips, executive director of The American Humane Association; actress
Julie Parrish accepting for Paramount Pictures; owner-trainer Frank
Inn, and Cat of Paramount's "Breakfast at Tiffany's," Picture Animal
Top Star of the Year.

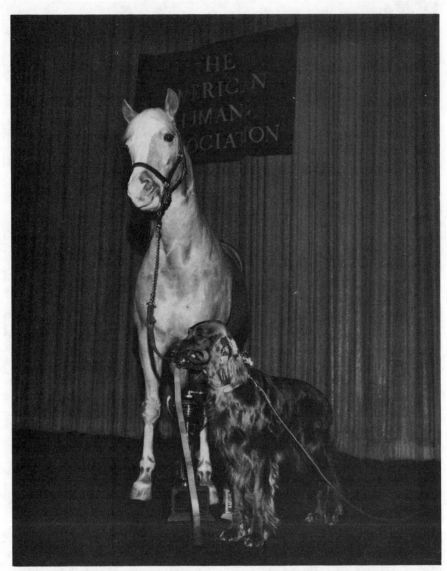

13th ANNUAL PATSY AWARDS: Picture Animal Top Star of the Year, Big Red. Performing Animal Television Star of the Year, Mister Ed.

PATSY WINNERS

Motion Pictures	Television
1951 Francis—mule California—horse Pierre—chimp	1958 Lassie—dog Cleo—dog Rin Tin Tin—dog
1952 Rhubarb—cat Francis—mule Cheta—chimp	1959 Lassie—dog Asta—dog Rin Tin Tin—dog
1953 Jackie—lion Bonzo—chimp Trigger—horse	1960 Asta—dog Lassie—dog Fury—horse } Jasper—dog } tie
1954 Sam—dog Francis—mule Jackie—lion	1961 Tramp—dog Lassie—dog Fury—horse
1955 Gypsy—horse Francis—mule Esmeralda—seal	1962 Mister Ed—horse Lassie—dog Tramp—dog
1956 wildfire—dog Francis—mule Faro—dog	1963 Mister Ed—horse Lassie—dog Tramp—dog
1957 Samantha—goose War Winds—horse Francis—mule	1964 Lassie—dog Mister Ed—horse Tramp—dog
1958 Spike—dog Beauty—horse Kelly—dog	1965 Flipper—porpoise Lassie—dog Mister Ed—horse
1959 Pyewacket—cat Tanka—horse Harry—rabbit	1966 Flipper—porpoise Lord Nelson—dog Higgins—dog
1960 Shaggy—dog Herman—pigeon North Wind—horse	1967 Judy—chimp Flipper—porpoise Arnold—pig

	Motion Pictures		*Television*

1961 King Cotton—horse
       Spike—dog
       Stubbs—monkey ⎫ tie
       Skip—dog   ⎭

1962 Cat—cat
       Pete—dog
       Flame—horse

1963 Big Red—dog
       Sydney—elephant
       Zamba—lion

1964 Tom Dooley—dog
       Pluto—dog
       Raunchy—jaguar

1965 Patrina—tiger
       Storm—dog
       Junior—dog

1966 Syn Cat—cat
       Clarence—lion
       Judy—chimp

1967 Elsa—lion
       Duke—dog
       Vindicator—steer

1968 Ben—bear
       Sir Tom—mountain lion
       Sophie—sea lion

1969 Albarado—horse

1968 Arnold—pig
       Ben—bear
       Clarence—lion

1969 Arnold—pig
       Timmy—chimp
       Lassie—dog